Clarence Earl Gideon
and the Supreme Court

CLARENCE EARL GIDEON
and the
SUPREME COURT

by Anthony Lewis

A new edition of *The Supreme Court and How It Works*

with a new Afterword by the author

A Vintage Sundial Book

Random House, New York

TO ELIZA

who read the manuscript

DAVID AND MIA

PHOTOGRAPH CREDITS: page 2, National Archives; page 13, Flip Schulke (from Black Star); page 14 top, Pictorial Parade; page 14 bottom, Charles Mack (from CBS News); page 15 top, Fred Ward (from Black Star); page 15 bottom, Wide World; page 16, Harris & Ewing.

First Vintage Sundial Edition, October 1972. Originally published by Random House, Inc., in 1966 as *The Supreme Court and How It Works*.

Library of Congress Cataloging in Publication Data

Lewis, Anthony, 1927-
    Clarence Earl Gideon and the Supreme Court.

    (Vintage sundial books, VS-7)
    First published in 1966 under title: The Supreme Court and How It Works.
    1. United States. Supreme Court
2. Gideon, Clarence Earl.   3. Right to counsel—United States
    I. Title.

KF8742.Z9L4   1972   347'.73'26   72-3156
ISBN 0-394-70807-5

CONTENTS

1. CLARENCE EARL GIDEON'S PETITION 3
2. THE WORLD'S MOST POWERFUL JUDGES 17
3. THE COURT CONSIDERS THE PETITION 35
4. ABE FORTAS TAKES THE CASE 44
5. THE RIGHT TO COUNSEL 59
6. THE BRIEF FOR GIDEON 78
7. GIDEON IN PRISON 94
8. THE OTHER BRIEFS 101
9. ARGUMENT BEFORE THE COURT 115
10. THE JUSTICES DECIDE 133
11. THE RESULTS OF GIDEON'S CASE 144
12. THE SUPREME COURT AND THE PEOPLE 155

Epilogue: RETRIAL 169

Afterword: 1972 181
*Bill of Rights
    and Fourteenth Amendment* 191
Glossary 193
Index 198

*Clarence Earl Gideon
and the Supreme Court*

In The Supreme Court of The United States
Washington D.C.

Clarence Earl Gideon
Petitioner

vs.

H. G. Cochran, Jr., as
Director, Divisions
of corrections State
of Florida

Petition for a writ
of Certiorari Directed
To The Supreme Court
State of Florida.

No. 890 Misc.

OCT. TERM 1961

U. S. Supreme Court

To: The Honorable Earl Warren, Chief
Justice of the United States

Comes now The petitioner, Clarence
Earl Gideon, a citizen of The United States
of America, in proper person, and appearing
as his own counsel. Who petitions this
Honorable Court for a Writ of Certiorari
directed to The Supreme Court of The State
of Florida. To review the order and Judge-
ment of the court below denying The
petitioner a writ of Habeus Corpus.

Petitioner submits That The Supreme
Court of The United States has The authority
and jurisdiction to review the final Judge-
ment of The Supreme Court of The State
of Florida The highest court of The State
Under sec. 344 (B) Title 28 U.S.C.A. and
Because The "Due process clause" of the

The first page of Clarence Earl Gideon's petition
to the Supreme Court.

CHAPTER 1

Clarence Earl Gideon's Petition

ON the morning of January 8, 1962, the postman delivered to the Supreme Court building in Washington a large brown envelope from Clarence Earl Gideon, prisoner number 003826, Florida State Prison, P.O. Box 221, Raiford, Florida. It was taken to a small room just inside the great white marble columns that stand at the front of the building and are so much admired by tourists. There a secretary looked at it and guessed right away, from the return address, what it was—a petition from a poor prisoner

3

asking the Supreme Court to get him out of jail. She went into the next room and put the envelope on the desk of an assistant clerk of the Supreme Court, Michael Rodak Jr.

It was part of Rodak's job to check the papers sent by men in prison and by other people who cannot afford to meet the usual rules for bringing a case to the Supreme Court. Ordinarily, when someone takes a case there, he must pay a filing fee of $100. He must also pay for the printing of forty copies of a pamphlet explaining the case. But a law passed by Congress makes an exception for persons who do not have enough money for the printing costs or the $100 fee. They only have to swear that they are "unable to pay such costs." Then they can go ahead *in forma pauperis*—a Latin phrase meaning "in the manner of a poor person."

The rules of the Supreme Court itself show special concern for these paupers' cases. Rule 53 allows a poor man to file just one copy of the petition, instead of forty, and says that the Court will not throw out his petition just because he makes some mistakes in preparing it without the help of a lawyer. Rule 53 also drops the requirement that papers presented to the Court must be printed. It says they should be typewritten "whenever possible," but in fact hand-written papers are accepted.

Gideon's were handwritten in pencil. They were

done in careful lettering on lined sheets of paper provided by the Florida prison. At the top of each sheet was a set of rules for the prisoners: "Only 2 letters each week . . . written on one side only . . . letters must be written in English." Gideon had filled seven pages. His spelling and punctuation were a bit peculiar, and he used lots of old-fashioned lawyers' phrases, such as "Comes now the petitioner . . ." It seemed that he must have been reading some old law books.

Rodak looked over the papers to see whether this prisoner had obeyed a few simple rules. For example, no *in forma pauperis* case can be accepted unless the person presenting it has formally sworn that he is too poor to pay the regular costs. Gideon's papers included the necessary oath. There is also a time limit on bringing cases to the Supreme Court from lower courts—ninety days for criminal cases. Gideon enclosed a paper showing that he had asked the Florida Supreme Court to free him and that the Florida court had rejected his plea on October 30, 1961, less than ninety days before.

Accordingly, Rodak stamped Gideon's papers with the date and gave his case a number, 890 Miscellaneous. That meant it was the 890th case on what the Court calls its Miscellaneous Docket, a group of cases made up mostly of pleas from poor prisoners—the 890th in the present term of the Court, which had begun the previous October. (The Supreme Court usually sits from October to June.) Rodak also gave the case a formal name, *Gideon v. Cochran,* Cochran being the man from whose control Gideon was trying to get free—H. G. Cochran Jr., director of the Florida prison system. Then Rodak put all the papers in a big red folder. (Red folders are used for these *in forma pauperis* cases on the Miscellaneous Docket, blue folders for the cases with regular printed papers.) He sent the folder down to the file room on an electric dumbwaiter.

There was very little in what he had sent to the Supreme Court to give a picture of Clarence Earl Gideon. In fact, he was a 51-year-old man who had been in and out of prisons since the age of fourteen. He had had a miserable life, and he looked it: His face was wrinkled, his voice and hands trembled, his body was frail. He had never been a vicious criminal, a gangster or a man of violence. He had no real education. He just could not seem to settle down to work, and so he made his way by gambling and occasional small thefts. Those who had known him, even the men who had arrested him and those who were now his jailers, considered Gideon a harmless if dejected human being, a man tossed aside by life, shipwrecked. He struck people meeting him for the first time as the most wretched of men.

And yet a flame still burned inside Clarence Earl

Gideon. He had not given up caring about life or freedom. Right now he had a fierce feeling that the State of Florida had treated him wrongly, unjustly, and he was determined to do something about that. Even in the formal language of his petition to the Supreme Court, his passion for justice could be sensed.

What was his case? Gideon said he had been sentenced to five years in prison for breaking into a building at night with the idea of stealing money—the Bay Harbor Poolroom in Panama City, Florida. He complained that at his trial he had been denied "due process of law." The Fourteenth Amendment to the Constitution of the United States says that no state shall take any man's "life, liberty or property without due process of law."

If Florida had taken away Gideon's liberty at a trial without "due process of law," he was certainly entitled to complain. But in what way was he saying that Florida had not given him "due process"? Here was his statement:

When at the time of the petitioners trial he ask the lower court for the aid of counsel, the court refused this aid. Petitioner told the court that this [Supreme] Court made decision to the effect that all citizens tried for a felony crime should have aid of counsel. The lower court ignored this plea.

Gideon's language was awkward, but his point was clear. What he was saying was that he should have had a lawyer at his side when he was tried—counsel to help in his defense against the charge that he had broken into the Bay Harbor Poolroom. Since he was too poor to pay a lawyer himself, the State of Florida should have given him one. To try a man for a felony —a serious crime—without a lawyer was to try him without "due process."

In other words, Gideon claimed that the Constitution, in the Fourteenth Amendment, guaranteed every poor man a free lawyer when he was put on trial for a serious crime. That was a simple and sensible-sounding argument. There was only one thing wrong with it. Just twenty years before, the Supreme Court had turned it down.

That was the famous case of *Betts v. Brady*. (Supreme Court cases generally carry the names of the two parties who are on the opposing sides, separated by *v.*, short for *versus* or "against." Betts in this case was a poor Maryland farmhand who had been convicted of robbery; Brady was the warden of the jail from which he was trying to get free.) In *Betts v. Brady*, in 1942, the Supreme Court ruled that "due process" did *not* require a lawyer to help every defendant facing a serious criminal charge. The ordinary man could take care of himself in a courtroom without a lawyer's help, the Court said.

According to the Court, the Constitution required a state to provide a lawyer for a poor man only if he suffered from some "special circumstance" that made it particularly hard for him to defend himself without a lawyer. For example, he might be sick. Or he might be so young or mentally backward that he could not understand the trial. Or it might be an unusually complicated case that only a lawyer could unravel. In these "special circumstances" the Supreme Court said that the states must supply lawyers for poor defendants—but not in the ordinary, run-of-the-mill case.

Gideon could have tried to show that he suffered from one of those "special" problems that would have entitled him to a lawyer. But he had not done so. From the day he was tried, Gideon had insisted on one idea: that under the Constitution of the United States he had an absolute right to be given a lawyer for his defense simply because he was a poor man and stood accused of a serious crime.

Gideon was tried on August 4, 1961, in the Circuit Court of the Fourteenth Judicial Circuit of Florida, covering Bay County and Panama City. The judge was Robert L. McCrary Jr., and the prosecutor was William E. Harris, an assistant state attorney. The record of the trial was taken down by a court stenographer. In the record, Judge McCrary is referred to as "The Court," Gideon as "The Defendant," and the stenographer as "The Reporter." The record begins as follows:

THE COURT: "The next case on the docket is the case of the State of Florida, Plaintiff, versus Clarence Earl Gideon, Defendant. What says the State, are you ready to go to trial in this case?"

MR. HARRIS: "The State is ready, your Honor."

THE COURT: "What says the Defendant? Are you ready to go to trial?"

THE DEFENDANT: "I am not ready, your Honor."

THE COURT: "Did you plead not guilty to this charge by reason of insanity?"

THE DEFENDANT: "No sir."

THE COURT: "Why aren't you ready?"

THE DEFENDANT: "I have no counsel."

THE COURT: "Why do you not have counsel? Did you not know that your case was set for trial today?"

THE DEFENDANT: "Yes sir, I knew that it was set for trial today."

THE COURT: "Why, then, did you not secure counsel and be prepared to go to trial?"

The Defendant answered the Court's question, but spoke in such a low tone that it was not audible.

THE COURT: "Come closer up, Mr. Gideon, I can't understand you, I don't know what you said, and the Reporter didn't understand you either."

At this point the Defendant arose from his chair

where he was seated at the counsel table and walked up and stood directly in front of the bench, facing his Honor, Judge McCrary.

THE COURT: "Now tell us what you said again, so we can understand you, please."

THE DEFENDANT: "Your Honor, I said: I request this court to appoint counsel to represent me in this trial."

THE COURT: "Mr. Gideon, I am sorry, but I cannot appoint counsel to represent you in this case. Under the laws of the State of Florida, the only time the court can appoint counsel to represent a Defendant is when that person is charged with a capital offense [one carrying the death penalty upon conviction, such as murder]. I am sorry, but I will have to deny your request to appoint counsel to defend you in this case."

THE DEFENDANT: "The United States Supreme Court says I am entitled to be represented by counsel."

THE COURT: "Let the record show that the defendant has asked the court to appoint counsel to represent him in this trial and the court denied the request and informed the defendant that the only time the court could appoint counsel to represent a defendant was in cases where the defendant was charged with a capital offense. The defendant stated to the court that the United States Supreme Court said he was

11

entitled to it."

Gideon was wrong, of course. The Supreme Court of the United States had not said he was entitled to a lawyer. In *Betts v. Brady* and other decisions it had said quite the opposite. It had said that a poor man had to show some special problem before the Constitution guaranteed him a lawyer for his defense. And Gideon had not claimed to be suffering from any special difficulty.

But that did not necessarily make Gideon's penciled letter to the Supreme Court a waste of time. For when the Supreme Court explains what the words of the Constitution mean—words such as "due process of law"—it does not bind itself for ever and ever; it does not pretend to be speaking with an absolute finality that must always be so. From time to time, after solemnly searching its own conscience, the Court decides that it has made a mistake in the past and over-rules—wipes out—one of its own decisions. Clarence Earl Gideon was calling for one of those great occasions in legal history. He was asking the Supreme Court to change its mind.

Clarence Earl Gideon

Abe Fortas

Bruce Robert Jacob

Chief Justice Earl Warren

Justice Hugo L. Black

*Nine men who might help Gideon: (seated, left to right)
Justices William O. Douglas, Hugo L. Black,
Earl Warren, Felix Frankfurter, and Tom C. Clark;
(standing) Charles E. Whittaker, John Marshall Harlan,
William J. Brennan Jr., and Potter Stewart.*

CHAPTER 2

The World's Most Powerful Judges

THE nine justices of the Supreme Court are the most powerful judges in the world. They decide, among other things, what kind of laws Congress may pass and what kind of orders the President may give —questions that would not be put to judges in other countries, where political leaders have the last word. Still, the Supreme Court is a court. It does its work in very much the same way as judges have done their job for centuries in England and the United States, and probably much the same way as they did in ancient Rome. To understand how the Supreme Court handled the case of Clarence Earl Gideon, it is important to know something about how all courts make and apply the law.

Courts exist to settle arguments. Before there were courts, disputes had to be resolved by force. One tribe carried on a feud with another. Or, in medieval times, there was a formal combat between two armored knights. Around 750 years ago in England, courts began to take the place of combat. People had come to see that it would be better to have disputes settled without violence, and settled according to some logical rules. Judges were sent out from London, traveling a circuit on horseback, to decide arguments and maintain "the King's peace." And they slowly started to develop the rules that we call law.

What happened was that a judge decided one dispute and then, when a somewhat similar case came along, said he must give the same answer as in the earlier one. This was called following *precedent*— following the rule made in the first case. It worked something like this: A man kept a ferocious dog inside a fence, but one day the dog got out and bit a neighbor. When the neighbor went to court, the judge decided that the owner was responsible and had to pay damages even though he had tried to keep the dog in by building the fence. In a later case a supposedly tame bear got out and killed a neighbor's chickens. The judge in that dispute looked back at the case of the ferocious dog and said he saw in it a good rule, a precedent—that someone who keeps dangerous animals must pay for their damage no matter how hard he tries to prevent injury. The precedent was applied to the case of the bear, and his owner had to pay for the chickens.

Gradually, as the judges decided more and more cases, a whole collection of precedents grew up, were collected in books and became known as "law." This judge-made law—the law of precedents, developed as courts tried to give fair answers to the many different problems brought before them—was called the Common Law.

Another kind of law came along later. This was made by representatives of the people gathered together in Parliament, and later in the assemblies of each American state and in the United States Congress. These assemblies elected by the people are called *legislatures*. They pass a law to change the rules made by the judges or to deal with some new problem that has not yet reached the judges in individual cases. For example, after the automobile was invented, it could have been left to the courts to decide over the years how fast it was reasonable to drive. Judges would have considered the problem every time there was an accident case and would gradually have worked out what was "speeding." But the

19

members of the legislature understandably felt that they did not want to wait until a lot of accidents happened and suits were brought, so they passed a general law providing for speed limits. This kind of law, made by a legislature, is called a *statute*.

Statutes, whether passed by Congress or the British Parliament or the California state legislature, still have to be applied in courts. It is a judge who says whether the law has been broken in a particular case. He interprets the statute—decides whether it was meant to cover this kind of case. In most places, for instance, there is a statute that forbids "reckless driving." But when Jones weaves his car in and out of traffic and is accused of "reckless driving," a judge —sometimes with the help of a jury—decides whether that was in fact "reckless." And so, today, "law" is made up both of *statutes* passed by legislatures and of *precedents* laid down by the courts in particular cases.

The Englishman or Frenchman lives under a single system of law—the law of England, the law of France. Not so the American. Our Constitution created a double system of governments, state and federal, each with its own law. A man who lives in New York State, for instance, is covered by both New York law and federal law, the law of the United States. He has to fill out a federal income tax return because of a statute passed by Congressmen in Washington. He also, with considerable annoyance, has to fill out a different New York State tax return because of a statute passed by members of the New York legislature in Albany.

Most of the law under which an American lives is the law of his state. His marriage, his property, his will are all governed by state law. If he gets into a lawsuit about a business contract or a real-estate deal or an automobile accident, the result will ordinarily be determined by state law—law laid down in state and local statutes and by the decisions of state courts.

The Constitution left it to the states to govern most of the daily life of the citizen. It gave the federal government power to deal with problems that really had to be handled centrally if anything was to get done. For example, the federal government has power over interstate commerce—over any business or transportation across state lines. For that reason, Congress can and does pass laws regulating interstate commerce. If a car thief steps into a Chrysler parked on East Eighty-seventh Street in Manhattan and drives it away, he violates the law of New York. If he drives the car across the George Washington Bridge into New Jersey, he also violates a federal law making it a crime to take stolen cars across state lines.

The existence of fifty different state governments and a central federal government is bound to lead to conflict. Two states may disagree, each wanting to apply its own law. Or there may be conflict between the federal government's policy and that of a state. There has to be some final authority to settle such clashes of conflicting law in a federal-state system. In the United States, from the very beginning of our history, this final referee has been the Supreme Court.

A famous early example was the steamboat case. In 1807 Robert Fulton built the first commercially successful boat worked by a steam engine, the *Clermont*. He and a partner, Robert R. Livingston, persuaded the New York State legislature to give them a monopoly—the exclusive right to run steamboats on the rivers in and around New York. One of those rivers is the great Hudson, which forms part of the boundary between New York and New Jersey. Fulton-Livingston boats did a thriving business going back and forth across the Hudson. The people of New Jersey naturally wanted to have some of that good business for themselves, and they were angry at New York's attempt to say who could and could not run steamboats on the Hudson. New Jersey passed its own steamboat law, and soon there were rival boats and even fights on the docks. Finally the New York boatmen brought a lawsuit to prevent anyone else from operating steamships on the Hudson.

The case went to the Supreme Court, and the decision was handed down by Chief Justice John Marshall—a man whose wisdom earned him the title of the Great Chief Justice. Marshall turned down the claims of the New York company. No state, he indicated, could grant a monopoly on a great avenue of commerce like the Hudson. The Constitution had given the job of regulating and encouraging interstate commerce to the federal government.

It is easy to see what might have happened to the United States if Chief Justice Marshall had allowed the New York monopoly to stand. Every state would have tried to grab its share of interstate commerce. There would have been gates at each state border— perhaps even customs inspectors. The United States, instead of developing into a unified, prosperous nation, would have been a collection of small, poor, quarreling states.

Thus one of the great purposes of the Supreme Court has been to hold the United States together as a Union. The Court is in a unique position to do so, because it sits alone at the top of the complicated structure of American law.

And it *is* complicated. In addition to having separate state and federal law, the United States has separate systems of courts. Each state has its own set of courts—trial courts, then the appellate courts that hear appeals from the trial judges, and usually a state supreme court. There is a similar system of federal courts, at least one court in every state. There are eighty-nine Federal District Courts (the trial courts) and eleven United States Courts of

Appeals, each in a circuit covering a section of the country. The First Circuit, for example, sits in Boston and decides appeals from all the federal courts in Massachusetts, Rhode Island, New Hampshire, Maine and Puerto Rico.

Only the Supreme Court of the United States hears appeals from all those different state and federal courts. The Supreme Court of California and the Supreme Judicial Court of Massachusetts may reach opposite decisions on some issue. Very often, too, the Massachusetts judges disagree with their friendly rivals just down the street, the federal judges of the United States Court of Appeals for the First Circuit. None of these courts can review each other's decisions. It is up to the United States Supreme Court to iron out the disagreements.

Nine men in Washington could not possibly go over the millions of lawsuits decided in the United States every year. Only a very few are reviewed by the Supreme Court—examined to see whether the lower courts decided them correctly. When someone tries to take his case to the Supreme Court, he must show that it is the kind of case the Court can and will consider.

Not every issue, nor every lawsuit, can legally be brought to the Supreme Court. It has a limited *jurisdiction*—the lawyers' word for the extent of a court's power. No court can make decisions effective beyond its jurisdiction. To take a very obvious example, a traffic-court judge in Chicago would have no effect if he strayed outside his jurisdiction one day and in a whimsical mood ordered the city of San Francisco to lower the fares on its cable cars. The jurisdiction of the Supreme Court is limited by the Constitution, by statutes of Congress and by rules laid down by the Court itself. The first question in the case of Clarence Earl Gideon, as in any case brought there, was whether it was within the Court's jurisdiction.

The Constitution defines and limits "the judicial power of the United States" in Article III. So far as the Supreme Court's jurisdiction goes, one basic limitation must be noted. The Court is given no power —absolutely no power—to change what state courts decide about *state* law. If farmer Smith in Eau Claire, Wisconsin, writes a will leaving his farm to a nephew but the Wisconsin courts rule that he did not properly sign it under Wisconsin law, that is the end of the case. The nephew cannot appeal to the Supreme Court.

For this reason the Supreme Court has nothing to do with the vast majority of cases decided by courts across the country. Most of those cases involve only issues of state law, such as the law of wills or property or automobile accidents. More than 10,000,000 cases are tried in American courts every year. Of these, no more than 300,000 are appealed at all, and only

2,500 or so are taken to the Supreme Court.

The cases that *are* within the Court's jurisdiction, that it can and does review, are those involving questions of *federal* law. Such a question would be the meaning of a statute passed by Congress. For example, Congress under its power to control interstate commerce has passed a law allowing railroad workers who are injured in accidents on the job to sue the railroad if the railroad was at fault. If a conductor steps off a stopped train in the dark, falls down a hill and breaks his leg, was the railroad "at fault" for stopping there? The Supreme Court would have jurisdiction to decide that question of the meaning of a federal law.

The other main kind of federal legal question that can reach the Supreme Court is the meaning of the Constitution itself. Again and again citizens claim that something has been done to them in violation of the Constitution—that, for instance, they have been convicted of a crime in a trial so unfair that it denied them "due process of law." That was Gideon's case.

The Gideon case illustrated a special complication in the complicated American legal machinery. It would be simpler for judges and law students and everyone else if state courts decided only matters of state law, and federal courts only federal matters. But that does not work. The two kinds of law get mixed up. Often when a state is trying a man on a

26

criminal charge, he says he is entitled to some protection from the Constitution, and then the state judge has to consider that question of federal law. That was exactly what had happened when Clarence Earl Gideon stood up in the courtroom in Florida and said that the Constitution entitled him to a lawyer.

The men who wrote the Constitution made clear that it was to be superior to state law and had to be followed by state courts. Article VI says: "This Constitution, and the Laws of the United States which shall be made in Pursuance thereof . . . shall be the Supreme Law of the Land; and the Judges in every State shall be bound thereby, any Thing in the Constitution or Laws of any State to the Contrary notwithstanding."

What was not so easily accepted was the idea that the United States Supreme Court should review the decisions of state judges on questions of federal law and tell those judges when they had gone wrong. This was regarded by some people as an insult to the independence of the states. In fact, in the year 1816, the judges of Virginia's highest court refused to obey a Supreme Court decision reversing what they had said in a case; they argued that the Court had no jurisdiction over them. The case went back to the Supreme Court, where Justice Joseph Story delivered a historic opinion reaffirming the Court's power to review state decisions on federal questions.

If there were no single high authority to control the often "jarring and discordant judgments" of different state courts and "harmonize them into uniformity," Justice Story said, then "the laws, the treaties and the Constitution of the United States would be different in different states. . . . The public mischiefs that would attend such a state of things would be truly deplorable."

All this goes to show that something that sounds as dry and technical as a court's jurisdiction may involve great issues of policy and power in the real world. Today, just as in Justice Story's day, state judges are likely to resent it when a decision of theirs is reversed in Washington. We have just gone through a period in which Supreme Court decisions on one subject—racial segregation and discrimination—have been strongly resisted by judges and politicians in one section of the country, the South. But President Kennedy and President Johnson gave their support to the Court, Congress passed laws to help carry out its decisions and the people as a whole recognized that the decisions must be obeyed, however difficult. History has settled the argument. The Supreme Court's authority to review state court decisions on the Constitution and other questions of federal law can no longer be doubted.

Gideon's case was, therefore, within the constitutional jurisdiction of the Supreme Court. In addition, he had met certain rules laid down by Congress: He had gone to the highest court of his own state—the Florida Supreme Court—and tried to get help there (unsuccessfully) before bothering the Supreme Court. He had filed his petition to the Supreme Court within ninety days after being turned down by the Florida court. In short, the claim that he was presenting to the Supreme Court was one that it *could* hear. Whether the Court *would* hear it was another matter.

Even with the limits on its jurisdiction, the Supreme Court gets many more cases than it has time to hear. Moreover, the justices do not like to be rushed into deciding difficult constitutional questions. They often prefer to let the hard questions wait until there has been time to get the ideas of lower courts and of legal experts writing in law reviews, the scholarly legal magazines usually edited by law students. For similar reasons, the Court will not ordinarily decide a question unless it is urgently raised by an actual case. A citizen who thinks it would be nice to know what the Supreme Court feels about some issue will not get an answer if he asks. President George Washington once wrote the justices a letter asking their advice on some points in a treaty he was arranging; they replied that they were sorry, but they could not answer such questions unless they arose in a real lawsuit.

"The most important thing we do is not doing,"

Justice Louis D. Brandeis used to say of himself and his colleagues on the Court. What he meant was that they had to take great care not to rush into decisions on constitutional questions. It is always a grave thing for the Court to say that a state or the federal government has violated the Constitution, and the justices must not do so lightly or casually. Several times in the past, the Supreme Court has become overexcited, rushed into a decision and turned out in the long run to be wrong. A notable example occurred just after the Civil War, when the Court ruled that it was unconstitutional for the government to issue paper money instead of gold and silver. A few years later the Court changed its mind and found paper money legal.

Justice Brandeis's point was that the justices have to have self-control in order to do their job. They have also needed some help from Congress to keep from being overwhelmed by the sheer number of cases. Early in this century the cases were coming in so fast that the Court could not cope with them and kept falling farther and farther behind. It took years to get a case decided. Worse yet, the justices were spending their energy on minor, unimportant cases that people had a right to bring before them, and there was little time left for the big constitutional questions.

Congress came to the rescue in 1925. It gave the

Supreme Court a new and vital power—the right to go through all the cases brought to it and pick out only the most important ones for decision. The other cases, though formally within the Court's jurisdiction, the justices could simply refuse to hear. For the person pressing a case, a new stage was added to the process of obtaining a Supreme Court decision: He first had to persuade the Court to hear the case at all.

Since 1925 one of the regular duties of the Supreme Court has been to decide which cases it will decide. This is how it works: If someone wants to take his case to the Supreme Court, he must first file a formal request to the Court to consider the case. This request is called a *petition for certiorari.* (The word *certiorari* is Latin, and even the justices do not entirely agree on how it should be pronounced. The Harvard Law School pronunciation is sersh-yo-RARE-eye.)

The Court may deny the petition. This means that the case has simply come to an end, and that the decision of the lower court stands.

Or the Court may grant the petition. It then issues a *writ of certiorari,* which is a formal order to bring a case up from a lower court for consideration. Lawyers on both sides of the case are given a chance to make a full argument to the justices, who later announce their decision.

Most petitions for certiorari are denied. In an

average year nowadays, 2,500 cases are brought to the Supreme Court. Of those, the Court selects no more than 150 for a full hearing.

There are no fixed rules for getting a case through this extremely tough process of selection. The justices ordinarily give no reasons for granting or denying a petition; if they had to, they would take so much time that the whole idea of lightening the pressure of cases would be defeated. But some reasons are obvious. When two lower courts have decided a significant question in exactly opposite ways, the chances are good that the Supreme Court will try to resolve their conflict. When the whole country is waiting for the answer to a legal question—as, for example when President Truman seized the country's steel mills to prevent a strike and the legality of his action was questioned—then the Supreme Court is likely to act. But there are never any guarantees about a petition for certiorari, because the nine justices do not drop any hints of what they will do; they discuss the matter among themselves and say nothing to the outside world until they announce whether they will review a case.

The only general guidance is that a petition is more likely to be granted if it raises a question important not only to the individuals in that case but to the whole country. Chief Justice Fred M. Vinson said in 1949 to a group of lawyers that when the Supreme

Court agreed to hear a case, the lawyer involved should realize that he represented not only his clients "but tremendously important principles, upon which are based the plans, hopes and aspirations of a great many people throughout the country."

Clarence Earl Gideon's petition for certiorari clearly met the test of importance. His claim that every poor man had a right to have a lawyer at his side when he was tried for a crime raised the most basic kind of constitutional question. If he succeeded, he would affect the rights of men in trials all over the country. The states would have to find new ways of getting enough lawyers for all those who could not afford to pay for one. A decision in Gideon's favor might even help men already in jail; if they had been tried and convicted without a lawyer, they might now have the right to a new trial with a lawyer's help.

But all these things that made the case of *Gideon v. Cochran* important also raised problems for the justices of the Supreme Court. It seemed likely, for example, that a decision for Gideon would annoy many states and increase criticism that the Court was injuring state independence. The possible effect on men already in jail would disturb many police officials around the country, and others concerned with crime. And there was the whole problem of whether it was wise for the Court to overturn one of its own decisions—*Betts v. Brady,* the 1942 ruling that poor men accused of crime did not have an absolute right to the assistance of counsel in their defense. There had been several earlier chances for the Court to upset *Betts v. Brady,* and it had not done so. In one case, Justice Felix Frankfurter had warned specifically of the possibility of "opening wide the prison doors of the land."

These were some of the thoughts, the pros and the cons, that must have been in the minds of the nine justices as Clarence Earl Gideon's case began working its way through the processes of the Supreme Court.

CHAPTER 3

The Court Considers the Petition

ONE of the outstanding qualities of the Supreme Court is the fact that it does its own work. We are in the age of Big Government and Big Business, when most officials have a large staff to help solve their problems and ghostwriters to write their speeches. The work at the Supreme Court is still done by nine men, assisted only by eighteen young law clerks.

The Court has no system of rank; no one man tells the others what to do, like a general in the Army.

Even the Chief Justice is only, as is said, "first among equals." He sits at the center of the bench and presides when the Court holds its sessions. But in the actual work of the Court his influence depends entirely on the respect that his eight colleagues have for his intelligence and his judgment. He has no power to order the others, only to persuade. Each justice has one vote, and it is in the keeping of his own mind and conscience.

The work is not parceled out to different panels or committees of justices. Every case is a matter for the whole court, and each justice is therefore responsible for every case—unless he stays out of a decision because, for example, it involves a member of his family. The nine men work mostly on their own, and the result is that there are nine separate law offices, with different ways of working. But it is possible to give a general picture of how the Court goes about its business from day to day.

The ordinary pleas to the Court to hear a case, the petitions for certiorari, are filed in the form of printed booklets. (The Court's rules fix an exact size, $6\frac{1}{8}$ inches by $9\frac{1}{4}$, but the paper cover may be any color. One big Washington law firm always uses beige, while others prefer a bold red; the federal government sticks to a conservative dark grey.) After someone has filed a petition for certiorari, the other side in the case has thirty days to answer. This answer, also in the form of a printed pamphlet, usually urges the Court not to hear the case.

Most justices use their law clerks to help handle the flood of petitions for certiorari. The clerk will study the petition and the answer in a case and write a memorandum for his justice outlining the issues presented.

Law clerks to the individual justices are not to be confused with the permanent employees in the office of the Clerk of the Supreme Court. The law clerks work for one justice personally, not for the whole Court, and only for a year or two. They are bright young men (or, very occasionally, women) recently out of law school, where they stood near the top of their class. Almost all federal and many state judges now have law clerks. The competition is keen among graduating law students for the honor of becoming a clerk, especially to a Supreme Court Justice. Many Supreme Court law clerks have gone on to fame as teachers or businessmen or public officials. Former Secretary of State Dean Acheson had once been clerk to Justice Brandeis, for instance, and Justice Byron R. White of the present Court clerked for the late Chief Justice Vinson. In addition to helping sift the petitions for certiorari, law clerks help in research and may write drafts of opinions. But the decision —what to do about a petition or an opinion— is always the justice's in the end.

Clarence Earl Gideon's petition for certiorari, as we have seen, was not one of the printed documents required by the rules for ordinary cases. It was a handwritten petition that he was seeking permission to file as a poor person. His case was accordingly handled in a somewhat different way. The Court has developed special procedures for the paupers' cases because of the special difficulties they present.

The papers filed by Gideon were held for thirty days in their red envelope to allow time for the other party to the case—Cochran, the head of the Florida prison system—to file a reply. (Cochran knew about Gideon's petition because, under the rules, Gideon had had to mail a copy to him.) But the authorities seldom bother to answer petitions from poor prisoners, and there was no reply to Gideon's within the thirty days. On February 8, 1962, the Gideon papers were sent from the file room to the office of Chief Justice Earl Warren.

The Chief Justice's law clerks have the special job of looking over the frequently confused, pathetic appeals from prisoners and preparing a memorandum on each case. This memorandum, indicating the facts and the legal issues as clearly as possible, is then circulated to all nine justices—along with the original petition by the prisoner if any justice wants to see it. If a law clerk thinks a prisoner has an interesting point that the Court might want to hear, he may suggest even before sending his memorandum around that the state authorities be asked specifically to answer the prisoner's petition. The hope is that this answer, written by trained lawyers, will clarify the murky picture that most prisoners give of their own cases.

This approach was followed in Gideon's case. On March 8, a month after the papers went to the Chief Justice's office, a letter was sent to the attorney general of Florida, Richard W. Ervin. It read in part:

RE: GIDEON V. COCHRAN
No. 890 Misc., October Term, 1961

Dear Sir:

On January 8, 1962, Clarence Earl Gideon, an inmate of the Florida State Prison, at Raiford, filed a petition for writ of certiorari in this Court. . . . Our records indicate that you have been served with a copy of the petition.

The Court has directed this office to request that you file a response to the petition. . . .

John F. Davis, Clerk
by *Michael Rodak Jr.*
Assistant

The response came in on April 9, signed by Attorney General Ervin and one of his assistants, Bruce R. Jacob. Its thirteen typewritten pages argued that the

Court should not hear Gideon's case. The argument rested on the precedent of *Betts v. Brady*, the 1942 decision in which the Supreme Court had held that the Constitution did not guarantee free lawyers to all poor men tried for crimes. Under *Betts v. Brady* a poor man had to be given a lawyer only if he suffered from some "special circumstances," such as youth or racial prejudice or mental backwardness, and Gideon had never claimed to be the victim of any such special difficulty. His only complaint was that he was poor. Thus, said the Florida lawyers, he must be given the same answer that the Supreme Court had given to Betts twenty years before: No.

A copy of that response went, under the rules, to Gideon. From the Raiford prison he sent a brief comment to the Court, four pages long, again in pencil.

"Petitioner cannot make any pretense at being able to answer the learned attorney general of Florida," Gideon began modestly, "because the petitioner is not attorney or versed in law nor does not have the law books to copy down the decisions of this Court."

But then, in his humble way, Gideon wrote a few very convincing lines. "It makes no difference," he said, "how old I am or what color I am or what church I belong to if any. . . . The question is very simple. I requested the court to appoint me attorney and the court refused. . . ." Gideon knew nothing about *Betts v. Brady,* but his words amounted to an effective criticism of that decision. The right to a lawyer to help in one's defense, he was saying, should not depend on complicated legal findings about the "special circumstances" in a case.

Now all the papers in the case of *Gideon v. Cochran,* together with a memorandum by one of the Chief Justice's law clerks, were circulated among the justices. By the end of May they were all ready to discuss the case, which was therefore put on their next conference list—a mimeographed list sent around before each formal conference of the Court so that the justices will know the cases to be discussed.

The nine justices meet formally in conference on Fridays, about three Fridays out of four during the October-June term. The conference room is an oak-paneled chamber next to the Chief Justice's office in the rear of the building. It is a plain room, with shelves and shelves of law reports and a long, heavy table in the middle. A single picture, of the Great Chief Justice, John Marshall, looks down at the justices seated around the table.

No one except the justices has ever been allowed into that room during the conference—no secretaries, no law clerks, no messengers. If a message arrives, the junior justice—the one most recently appointed —goes to the door to get it. The secrecy has two purposes. It keeps news of the decisions from leaking

41

out ahead of time, and it assures the justices that they can talk to each other in complete frankness without having to worry about being quoted around town.

The conference starts at 10:00 A.M. and usually runs on until the late afternoon. At the start each justice, when he enters the room, shakes hands with all the others there (thirty-six handshakes altogether). The conference first takes up the petitions for review. Then the justices consider the cases on which they have heard formal argument in court that week, and they take a first vote on who should win those cases.

The Chief Justice starts the discussion of each matter. The senior associate justice—Hugo L. Black at the time of the Gideon case—speaks next, and so on down the line. Voting is in reverse order, with the junior justice first and on up to the Chief Justice. It takes only four votes out of nine to grant a petition of certiorari. The Court evidently reasons that if that many members think a case is important, the majority should be willing at least to hear the case argued.

At the conference of June 1, 1962, the Supreme Court had dozens of cases before it. There were several obviously weighty matters, such as the long-standing dispute between the states of Arizona and California about their rights to water from the Colorado River. (The justices decided to hear some more argument about that complicated case the next fall.) There was one case of racial discrimination, and there was a labor dispute. And the justices also passed on the handwritten petition for certiorari filed by Clarence Earl Gideon.

The results of this conference were made known to the world shortly after 10:00 A.M. the following Monday, June 4, 1962, when the Supreme Court's orders for that day were posted on a bulletin board. One order read:

890 Misc. GIDEON V. COCHRAN

The motion for leave to proceed *in forma pauperis* and the petition for writ of certiorari are granted. In addition to other questions presented by this case, counsel are requested to discuss the following in their briefs and oral argument:

"Should this Court's holding in *Betts v. Brady* be reconsidered?"

CHAPTER 4

Abe Fortas
Takes the Case

WHEN it agrees to review the case of a poor prisoner, the Supreme Court quickly appoints a lawyer to argue the case for him. Such an appointment is a great honor for the lawyer selected. It may also require great personal sacrifice. The only pay for weeks of work is the satisfaction of performing a service for the country. If the lawyer lives at a distance from Washington, the Court pays his railroad or airplane fare, but he gets nothing for a hotel room or a secretary or other expenses. The Court has no fixed rules for appointing counsel but naturally tends to pick lawyers known personally or by reputation to one or more of the justices. It might be a young man just starting out, perhaps a recent law clerk, or it could be someone as prominent as former Secretary of State Acheson, who was appointed a few years ago to represent a Texas prisoner.

The justices discussed the question of a lawyer to argue Gideon's case at their conference of Friday, June 22, 1962. That turned out to be the last conference of the term that had begun in October, 1961; the following Monday the Court handed down all its remaining opinions, including a controversial one about prayers in New York public schools, and recessed for the summer. Shortly after the conference ended that Friday evening, Chief Justice Warren called in the Clerk of the Supreme Court, John F. Davis—the Court's top permanent staff member, not to be confused with the justices' law clerks. The Chief Justice told Davis that the conference had chosen Abe Fortas, of Washington, D.C., to argue Gideon's case, and asked Davis to telephone Fortas and tell him of his selection. (Lawyers are always privately informed before their appointment is announced, in case they feel that they cannot take on the job. But selection by the Supreme Court to represent a poor man is a little like a President's invitation to dinner: It is almost never refused.)

Fortas turned out to be in Dallas, Texas. Davis reached him there and told him about the case—briefly, but explaining the important point that the Court had agreed to re-examine its 20-year-old decision limiting poor criminal defendants' right to counsel, *Betts v. Brady*. Fortas said he would be happy to argue the case for Clarence Earl Gideon.

Abe Fortas was a high-powered example of a high-powered type, the Washington lawyer. At the time of his appointment he was just fifty-two years old. He came from the background of a Jewish family in the South—in Memphis, Tennessee, where he was born on June 19, 1910. He went to a small college in Memphis, Southwestern College, and from there to the much tougher and more competitive world of the Yale Law School. He showed that he had the intelligence and the will power to compete in that world by becoming editor-in-chief of the *Yale Law Journal*. After graduation, in 1933, he went to Washington and worked for the New Deal government of President Franklin D. Roosevelt. One of his chiefs was William O. Douglas, who had been a professor of his at Yale and who was soon—in 1939—to move on to the Supreme Court himself. At the young age of thirty-two, in 1942, Fortas became Undersecretary of the Interior.

He left the government in 1946 to go into the private practice of law. Soon he was the driving force in a new Washington law firm, Arnold, Fortas and Porter. He became known especially for his exceptional skill at arguing cases in the courtroom—a skill that most lawyers neglect, preferring to work quietly in their own offices on written material. He also took an active part in advising several large businesses and was always flying around the country to their meetings. More than most lawyers he was interested in the rights of men charged with crimes. He had been named by Chief Justice Warren to a committee that was working to improve the rules for handling criminal cases in the federal courts. He was concerned about the little man who found himself on trial, but not just because he was sorry for the particular man. Rather, he was convinced that it was good for everyone in the country to have a system of justice that treated people fairly. A friend said he was "an angry man—angry at injustice." His wife was an outstanding lawyer, too, an expert on taxes who practiced under her maiden name, Carolyn Agger.

Fortas was a rather small man with a slow but extremely forceful way of speaking. He never seemed to say or do anything by accident; he planned carefully. His house and his office were filled with beautiful antique furniture and with old and new works of art. He liked to play the violin in his spare time, and he was a good friend of many musicians, including the great cellist Pablo Casals. He knew several members of the Supreme Court; undoubtedly one of them had suggested his appointment in the Gideon case. He was also an old friend of, and lawyer for, Vice President Lyndon B. Johnson. (Three years later, long after the Gideon case and after the murder of President Kennedy, President Johnson made Abe Fortas a justice of the Supreme Court.)

The first thing Fortas had to do as lawyer for Clarence Earl Gideon in the Supreme Court was to learn about Gideon's case. He sent a young man in his law firm up to the Court to look over the papers in the case and make copies of them, but these did not tell Fortas or the others in his firm very much. There were only Gideon's vaguely worded petition, Florida's response and Gideon's reply to that. These were enough to demonstrate the big legal question that the justices had seen in the case: the right of a poor man to have a lawyer's help when he is on trial for his life or liberty. The actual facts of this particular case—of Gideon's life, of the crime he was supposed to have committed, of his trial and imprisonment—might be thought to make no difference to that issue before the Supreme Court. But it is against the tradition of our law for lawyers to argue or courts to decide great issues as bare theories, without any facts about the people involved. A lawyer wants the sense of flesh and blood; he wants a human being for a client, not a theory.

Moreover, it is the duty of a lawyer to win for his client on any possible ground. If Fortas learned more about the case, he might find that Gideon was suffering from mental illness or some other "special circumstance" that should have given him a lawyer even under the narrow old rule of *Betts v. Brady*. If so, Fortas would have to present that fact to the Supreme Court and ask the Court to set aside the conviction without ever reconsidering the Betts case. That would wash out the chance of taking a great step in the law—of extending the right to counsel to criminal trials all across the country. But the Supreme Court does not like to take such big steps unless it absolutely has to, unless there is no lesser way to deal with a case. The justices look with suspicion on a lawyer who becomes so eager to make a great change in the law that he forgets about simpler ways of winning the case for his client.

For these reasons Fortas decided to get the exact record of what had happened at Gideon's trial—the transcript as taken down by the court stenographer in Panama City, Florida. This was arranged by the Clerk's office at the Supreme Court, which sent down to Florida for a copy and passed it on to Fortas. The transcript made interesting reading.

Gideon was tried on August 4, 1961, by Judge Robert L. McCrary Jr. and a jury. Usually the two

lawyers on opposite sides start out with speeches telling the jury what they expect to prove. In this case,
after Gideon's unsuccessful attempt to get a lawyer,
the prosecutor, William E. Harris, made his speech.
Then the judge let Gideon address the jury. "Just
walk right around there where you can see them,"
Judge McCrary said, "and tell them what you expect
the evidence to show in your favor. Talk loud enough
for them to hear you, now." After this, prosecutor
Harris read to the jury the formal charge against
Gideon: that he had broken into the Bay Harbor
Poolroom on the morning of June 3, 1961, in order
to steal a small amount of money and property.

The main witness for the prosecution was someone
named Henry Cook. He took the stand and said he
was outside the Bay Harbor Poolroom at 5:30 A.M.
on that June third and saw Gideon inside. After
watching through the window for a few minutes,
Cook testified, he saw Gideon come out with a pint
of wine in his hand, make a telephone call at the
street corner and get into a taxi. Then, said Cook, he
looked into the poolroom again and saw that it
"had been broken into." The front was off a cigarette
machine, and its money box was lying on a pool table.

After the prosecution calls a witness and brings out
his testimony by questions, the defense gets its turn
to cross-examine—to ask the witness questions that
may weaken the effect of what he has said for the

prosecution. Gideon, acting as his own lawyer, tried briefly to cross-examine Cook. Most of his questioning seemed to have no real point.

"Do you know positively that I was carrying a pint of wine?" he asked Cook once.

"Yes, I know you was."

"How do you know that?"

"Because I seen it in your hand."

Gideon did ask what Cook was doing outside the poolroom at 5:30 in the morning. That could have been an interesting question to follow up, because a jury might well think there was something suspicious about a man hanging around a poolroom at that hour. But when Cook replied that he had "just come from a dance down in Apalachicola, stayed out all night," Gideon dropped the subject. He did not ask Cook his age, or what he did, or whether he had any reason to dislike Gideon—all matters that a lawyer would surely have explored.

The only other witness for the prosecution was the operator of the Bay Harbor Poolroom, Ira Strickland Jr., who said he found a window smashed when he arrived later that morning, and a cigarette machine and juke box broken into. Strickland said some coins were missing—he did not know how much money— and "a small amount of beer and some wine."

Gideon called eight witnesses for the defense. The first was the policeman who had discovered the break-in at the Bay Harbor Poolroom on June 3, 1961, Henry Berryhill Jr. He was just driving by in a patrol car, he said, when he saw the front door open. He "checked with a fellow at the front of the building, a Mr. Cook, and he said he saw you leave the building." Gideon did not ask what patrolman Berryhill thought Cook was doing "at the front of the building" at that hour.

It was unclear just why Gideon had called a policeman as his witness. The other witnesses he called were just as puzzling. There were a deputy sheriff who had investigated the break-in, the cab driver who picked Gideon up that morning and various persons from the neighborhood. Gideon did not ask them any questions that could have established an alibi or otherwise helped his defense. He asked one woman whether she had bought him a drink in the poolroom the night before, and she answered, "I probably did, if you needed one." That did not seem to have much to do with the case.

Under English and American law the defendant does not have to answer questions at his own trial, and Gideon chose not to take the witness stand. And so the trial came quickly to an end. The jury found Gideon guilty. Judge McCrary delayed the sentencing for three weeks so that he could get a report on Gideon's past history. On August 25, without any argument by Gideon (or, of course, by a lawyer for him), the judge gave him the highest possible sentence for breaking into the poolroom—five years in prison.

When Abe Fortas and his legal colleagues read that transcript, they no longer had any doubt that they should make the Gideon case a direct attack on the old rule that only poor men in "special circumstances" had to be given a lawyer under the Constitution. Plainly Gideon was not mentally backward or ill or a mere boy. The judge had tried to be fair. In short, Gideon had not suffered from any of the special disadvantages that would have entitled him to a lawyer under the old rule of *Betts v. Brady*. And yet it was completely clear that a lawyer would have helped. The trial had been rushed through, with a thin prosecution case. Gideon had not made a single objection or pressed any of the possibly favorable lines of defense. A young associate of Abe Fortas said later: "We knew as soon as we read that transcript that here was the perfect case to challenge the whole idea of *Betts v. Brady* that the ordinary man can have a fair trial without a lawyer. Gideon did very well for a layman, he acted like a lawyer. But it was a pitiful effort really. He may have committed this crime, but it was never proved by the prosecution. A lawyer—not a great lawyer, just an ordinary lawyer—could have made ashes of the case."

The transcript thus answered one of the big questions in Fortas's mind. But his curiosity was still not completely satisfied. The record of the trial had not told him very much about Clarence Earl Gideon the man. Fortas wondered whether he had been in prison before, whether he was white or Negro, what his education had been. Fortas thought about going down to Florida to visit Gideon in the prison to find out more, but he decided that he did not want to get so personally involved. Then chance gave him another way to get the information.

On August 1 Gideon began writing to Fortas. The Supreme Court had told him about Fortas's appointment to represent him, and he wondered what was going on. Fortas wrote back that he need not worry; but Gideon was still, understandably, a little nervous. On October 29 he wrote: "I guess I am impatient but it seems to take a long time. . . . If there is any information that I might be able to give you that will help the case I will give it." That gave Fortas an opening. He replied that "as a matter of my own interest" he would like to have a "careful and detailed" autobiography from Gideon, his life story: "when and where you were born, education, employment, family arrests. . . . I know that you will be extremely careful to be absolutely accurate. . . ."

The answer arrived in Washington on November 13. It was a letter of twenty-two pages, once again written by Gideon in pencil. It was a remarkable letter—honest and simple and moving. In the excerpts that follow, some of Gideon's curious spelling and punctuation have been changed slightly to make things clear.

"You will understand," Gideon wrote, "that due to my limited education and also to the utter folly and hopelessness of parts of my life, it will be doubtful if I can put it down on paper with any reasonable comprehension. I will not be proud of this biography. . . .

"I was born August 30th, 1910, in Hannibal, Missouri. My parents were Charles Roscoe Gideon and Virginia Gregory Gideon. My father died a few days after I was three years old. Mother remarried when I was five. . . .

"My step-father never could accept me or I could not accept him. My mother was very strict and my life as a child was of the strict discipline. My parents lived by the best moral customs and were members of the Calvary Baptist church Hannibal Mo. which I joined when I was about thirteen years of age. My mother still to this day has done nothing that could be classed as wrong. . . .

"I suppose I am what is called an individualist, a person who will not conform. Anyway my parents were always quarreling and I would be the scapegoat of those quarrels. My life was miserable. I was never allowed to do the things of an ordinary boy.

"At the age of fourteen I ran away from home, I accepted the life of a hobo and tramp in preference to my home. . . . My mother found out where I was at and she came and got me. Had me placed in the jail at Hannibal which I escaped from the next day and went back to the country to hide out. At this time it was extremely cold weather, and a short time later I burglarized a country store for some clothes which I was caught the next day by the store owner with all the clothes on. I was tried in Juvenile Court in Ralls County, Missouri. My mother asked the court to send me to the reformatory, which they did for a term of three years. Of all the prisons I have been in that was the worst. I still have scars on my body from the whippings I received there. . . ."

Gideon went on to describe a life that had gone downhill from there. He got out of the reformatory on parole at the age of 16 and went to work in a shoe factory at two dollars a day. Two years later, in 1928, he "committed some crimes" and was sent to a Missouri prison for burglary. After another try in a shoe factory he went to a federal prison for stealing from a federal armory. On getting out "I done the same as always" and was again convicted of burglary. In 1943 he escaped from prison in Missouri and went to work as a railroad brakeman, only to be turned in after a year or so. There was one more burglary conviction, in Texas in 1951. Then Gideon drifted.

He was in hospitals several times with troubles in his chest, including tuberculosis. He worked on fishing boats and tugboats. He was an electrician. Mostly he gambled, hanging around gambling joints and playing in small card games. He married four times. He and his last wife had three children, two boys and a girl, aged six and five and three when he wrote Fortas.

Finally Gideon and his family moved to the small town of Panama City, in the western panhandle of Florida. There, as he described it, things continued to go wrong for him. His wife began drinking. Because of his criminal record and because of an argument with the local sheriff, he said, the police began picking on him and arresting him for no reason. His health failed again, and he went to a hospital where he was treated wonderfully: "chicken every day. Can you imagine how I felt every time I ate my meals of steak and chicken when I would think of my children hoping they had anything at all."

Gideon admitted many crimes, but he told Fortas he was innocent of breaking into the Bay Harbor Poolroom. He suggested that he was the victim of a plot by others. He wandered on in the letter about what he called his mistreatment by Florida officials. He said he was fighting to keep the officials from taking his three children away from him. Then he ended as follows:

I have no illusions about law and courts or the people who are involved in them. I have read the complete history of law ever since the Romans first started writing them down, and before of the laws of religions. I believe that each era finds an improvement in law, each year brings something new for the benefit of mankind. Maybe this will be one of those small steps forward. . . . Thank you for reading all of this. Please try to believe that all I want now from life is the chance for the love of my children, the only real love I have ever had.

Sincerely yours
Clarence Earl Gideon

CHAPTER 5

The Right to Counsel

"THE question is very simple. I requested the court to appoint me attorney and the court refused." That is what Gideon had written to the Supreme Court, and many Americans would have agreed with him. It was only fair, they might have thought, to give a poor man a lawyer when you put him on trial. The Constitution certainly must have something to say about fair trials, and so the Supreme Court should just see to it that Gideon was given a lawyer.

But few of the problems given to the Supreme Court to settle are simple. This one—the right to counsel—had a long and complicated history behind it. Judges and senators and even Presidents had debated issues that were involved in the Gideon case. The Supreme Court justices who were to decide the case could not ignore that past. They could not just feel sorry for Clarence Earl Gideon and say: "He wins." As judges they had to worry not only about Gideon but about the larger questions raised by history. These were some of those questions:

Was it right for nine Supreme Court justices to tell the whole country what must be done for a poor man on trial? Or would it be more "democratic" to leave the problem to the people's elected representatives in Congress and the states?

Twenty years earlier the Supreme Court had decided that not all poor defendants were entitled to lawyers. Should the Court now be free to change its mind?

Should there be one rule about lawyers-for-the-poor covering the whole United States, or should each of the fifty states be allowed to make up its own mind?

In a way, the first of those questions—on the power of the nine justices—is the most important. Americans have come to take it for granted that the Supreme Court has the power to find the actions of governors and Congressmen and even Presidents unconstitutional. But this great power of *judicial review,* as it is called, is not given in the same way to judges in other lands. Most courts decide personal disputes about money or property. The Supreme Court of the United States decides, in the form of lawsuits, some of the largest issues facing the country. May the President seize the steel mills to prevent a strike? May white and Negro children be segregated in separate schools? The Supreme Court decides.

All this power gives the nine justices heavy responsibility. The burden is the heavier because they so often have the last word. Deciding cases is never easy, but a judge may sleep more soundly after sentencing a prisoner to death if he knows that there is an appeal to some other court. There is no appeal from the Supreme Court. Just a few months before the Court agreed to hear Gideon's case, one justice— Charles E. Whittaker—retired after only five years there because he found the strain of making such important decisions too great. He told friends that when he wrote an opinion, he felt as if he were carving his words into stone.

Some men have criticized the Supreme Court's great power as being opposed to the democratic idea of American government—the idea that the people should decide. After all, the critics argue, the justices are appointed by the President, not elected. They can serve for life, and they do not have to answer to voters. Why should they be allowed to decide whether elected officials have violated the Constitution?

In answer, people supporting the Supreme Court have made the point that our Constitution was precisely intended to keep elected officials from going too far. Freedom of speech and press and religion and the other great guarantees in the Constitution must be upheld when officials or even a majority of the people want to brush them aside. The Supreme Court is doing that essential job.

The argument has been going on for more than 160 years—since Chief Justice Marshall, in the case of *Marbury v. Madison* in 1803, first held that a statute passed by Congress violated the Constitution. President Thomas Jefferson denounced Marshall for that decision. Later justices have been criticized by first one side, then another—by liberal Northerners, for instance, in the 1930's when the Supreme Court stopped some of President Franklin Roosevelt's plans to help the poor; by conservative Southerners in the 1950's when the Court ruled against racial segregation.

Nowadays it is no longer worth arguing against the Supreme Court's power of judicial review. The Court has been telling Americans what the Constitution means, and making officials obey it, for so long that everyone depends on the Court. Our system could hardly work otherwise. But there is still a real argument about how the Court should use this great power, and how often. Should it be bold, reading the old words of the Constitution in large new ways so as to strike down any injustice in American life? Or should it be cautious, leaving problems to be settled by the states and the federal government except in the most urgent cases?

The two sides of that argument, as it happened, had famous champions inside the Supreme Court itself when the Gideon case came there. On one side was Justice Hugo L. Black, on the other Justice Felix Frankfurter. They had been on the Court together for nearly twenty-five years, and now they were both in their seventies. They were not enemies personally, but their disagreement about how to do their job seemed to grow hotter over the years.

Justice Frankfurter took the cautious view. He argued that in a democracy like the United States, the people usually had to improve things themselves —by their vote. If a state had an unfair law, it was up to the people to make their representatives change that law—or else to elect new representatives. The people should not leave it to nine justices in Washington to fix things up. Those justices might read the Constitution in a foolish way—indeed, they sometimes had in the past. Then everyone was stuck with that foolish rule unless the people went through the trouble of amending the Constitution or the Supreme Court reversed itself.

Of course, Justice Frankfurter did not say that the Supreme Court should never do anything. When he found a violation of the Constitution, he did not hesitate to say so. For example, he joined his colleagues in 1954 in unanimously ruling that it was unconstitutional to separate children in schools by their color. He just thought the Court should be slow to find laws unconstitutional. Often this attitude made him approve things as a justice that he personally did not like. When the government sent some Communists to jail in the 1950's for making speeches, Justice Frankfurter personally thought that the law was unwise and that Communists should be allowed to speak freely. But Congress had decided that Communist speeches were dangerous, and Justice Frankfurter did not think it was right for him to upset that Congressional decision. He upheld as constitutional the law under which the Communists were jailed.

Justice Black, on the contrary, thought it was wrong for the Supreme Court to worry too much about what state officials or Congressmen thought. In his view, the men who wrote the Constitution decided that the freedom of the individual person must be protected from officials who restrict that freedom. Therefore, the Supreme Court should be bold in striking down what officials do. It should not hesitate to find a law unconstitutional, and it should read the words of the Constitution in a large, generous way, not narrowly. When the Constitution talks about freedom of speech, Justice Black would say it means freedom for *all* speech, no matter how unpopular it may be or how much Congress may dislike it. He naturally *dissented*—disagreed with the majority— when the Supreme Court let the Communists be sent to jail for their speeches.

Justice Black was a bold legal thinker in one way that mattered directly to the Gideon case. He was readier than most judges to wipe out past decisions when he thought they were wrong. That is, he cared less about precedent—about following what was decided in earlier cases.

Law in Britain and the United States is built on the general assumption that courts will stick to what they have said in the past. Men sign contracts on that assumption, and write wills, and plan their businesses.

But American courts, unlike British, are not absolutely bound to follow precedent. They can reconsider what they have said before. That is especially true when the Supreme Court decides what the Constitution means, because it would be dangerous to freeze the ideas of one day's judges into the Constitution permanently. For example, judges who decided a hundred years ago what the Constitution meant about "interstate commerce" had never heard of telephones or automobiles or airplanes, and judges today have to reconsider the whole picture of commerce in light of those inventions. In constitutional cases, Justice Brandeis said, "this Court has often overruled its earlier decisions. The Court bows to the lessons of experience and the force of better reasoning."

Approximately one hundred times in its 175-year history the Supreme Court has reversed one of its past decisions. Still, there are strong arguments against doing that too often. People want to know where they stand; they do not want the law bobbing up and down likes horses on a merry-go-round. For this reason, many think it is better for the Supreme Court to stick to an old decision even though it now looks a little wrong. Justice Frankfurter felt strongly that way. He thought the law should respect history. He was more hesitant than Justice Black to abandon a precedent—a precedent such as *Betts v. Brady,* the 1942 case rejecting the same claim for a lawyer that Gideon was now making.

Another disagreement between Justices Black and Frankfurter cut even closer to Gideon's case. This was their view of *federalism*—the independence of the states in our system of government.

The Constitution, as we have seen, set up two levels of government in the United States, state and federal. Ever since then there has been disagreement about how much each state should be allowed to do on its own. A century ago the dispute erupted into Civil War, when the Southern States of the Confederacy demanded the right to leave the United States altogether. The Civil War settled that they had no such right, that the union of states was permanent. But the states, Northern as well as Southern, continued to do many things their own way.

Today state officials talk about "states' rights." By that they mean the right to handle such things as race relations and criminal law as they wish, without regulation by the federal Constitution or federal judges.

The cry of "states' rights" has sometimes aroused great emotion. And the Gideon case involved something about which state officials were especially sensitive—the right to deal with suspected criminals in their own way, without following national rules. Clarence Gideon was, after all, asking the Supreme Court to make all the states follow one national rule on the right to counsel in criminal trials. He was therefore bound to run into resistance from those who believed the states should be free to apply their own rules.

Justice Frankfurter was a strong believer in the independence of the states. Of course he did not think that the states were always wise or fair. But he thought one of the great things about the United States was that it had fifty different places where people could experiment with different ways of handling problems. To try to run everything from Washington, he felt, would dampen new ideas. He therefore resisted attempts in the Supreme Court to make the states all obey the same constitutional rules as the federal government. Justice Black, by contrast, thought the rules should be the same all over the country. He suspected that the states were abusing their independence by treating individuals like Clarence Earl Gideon unfairly.

This difference between Justices Black and Frankfurter focused for years on one large question: Should the Bill of Rights be applied to the states as well as the federal government?

The Bill of Rights is the name given to the first ten amendments to the Constitution, all proposed by the first Congress in 1789 and approved by the states in 1791. These amendments contain the guarantees of human liberty that are so familiar to freedom-loving people everywhere. The First Amendment, for example, assures freedom of speech, press, religion and assembly. The Fourth Amendment protects people's homes against unreasonable searches and seizures by government officials. The Sixth Amendment guarantees suspected criminals the right to counsel and to trial by jury.

But the Bill of Rights originally covered only the *federal government*. The First Amendment, for instance, said: "*Congress* shall make no law . . . abridging the freedom of speech . . ." It said nothing about what the states could do. The Supreme Court decided specifically in 1833 that the Bill of Rights limited only federal laws and the actions of federal officials. The Constitution did not prevent a state from abridging free speech or taking away the right to trial by jury in criminal cases.

Then came the Civil War. Afterward the country adopted a series of constitutional amendments to make sure no *state* could mistreat individual citizens. The Thirteenth Amendment prohibited slavery. The Fourteenth was written in much more general language, evidently designed to give the individual broader protection from unfairness on the part of state governments. It said in part: "No State shall . . . deprive any person of life, liberty or property without due process of law; nor deny to any person . . . the equal protection of the laws."

Soon it was being argued, in the Supreme Court and elsewhere, that those who wrote the Fourteenth Amendment had intended those vague phrases, such as "due process of law," to be a kind of shorthand for the whole Bill of Rights. In other words, it was said, the Fourteenth Amendment was intended to make the states follow exactly the same constitutional rules as the federal government.

Justice Black was the strongest believer in that

argument. In 1947, in *Adamson v. California*, he almost persuaded the Supreme Court to apply the whole Bill of Rights to the states—almost, but not quite. He lost by a vote of five to four, with Justice Frankfurter the strongest voice on the other side. That was the end of what is called the *incorporation* argument, for bringing the whole Bill of Rights into the Fourteenth Amendment as a limitation on action by the states.

But if that incorporation approach has failed, another has worked. This has been for the Supreme Court to apply various parts of the Bill of Rights to the states one by one. The Court has done this by means of the Fourteenth Amendment's guarantee of "due process of law." If a state takes away any "fundamental" right listed in the Bill of Rights, the Court has said, the state is denying "due process of law." For example, freedom of speech is protected by the First Amendment against abridgment by Congress. It is so central to human liberty, the Supreme Court has said, that it is also protected by the Fourteenth Amendment. A state that denies a man freedom of speech has violated the Fourteenth Amendment by depriving him of liberty without due process of law.

The hard part has been to decide which guarantees in the Bill of Rights are so "fundamental" that they should be included in "due process." At first the Supreme Court was reluctant to include any. As late as the year 1922 it said that the protections of the First Amendment—of speech, press, religion and assembly—did not apply to the states. But in 1925 the Court changed its mind and said free speech was fundamental and could not be denied by the states without violating the Fourteenth Amendment. The other freedoms of the First Amendment followed.

The justices were extremely hesitant to apply to the states those portions of the Bill of Rights dealing with the procedure at criminal trials. Most of them seemed to feel, as Justice Frankfurter did, that the states should have independence above all in the handling of crime. Year after year the Court rejected claims that the states should have to follow the Bill of Rights on such matters as trial by jury in criminal cases.

A key case was decided in 1949, *Wolf v. Colorado*. It concerned the Fourth Amendment's ban on unreasonable police searches. For many years it had been the rule in federal courts that something found in an illegal search could not be used as evidence against a man at his trial. Now the Supreme Court was asked to make the states follow the same rule. The Court refused, explaining that it thought the states should be allowed to go their own way in this area. Justice Frankfurter wrote the opinion.

The provision of the Bill of Rights that was crucial in Gideon's case was this part of the Sixth

Amendment: "In all criminal prosecutions, the accused shall enjoy the right . . . to have the Assistance of Counsel for his defense."

When that amendment was adopted, back in the eighteenth century, it was not aimed at the problem of poor men. Instead, it was intended to prevent Congress from adopting an old English practice that barred lawyers even for criminal defendants who could afford them. It was not until 1836 that the English Parliament passed a law letting *any* defendant hire his own counsel.

Over the years in the United States "the right to counsel" came more and more to mean a man's right to have a lawyer for his defense whether he could afford it or not. The criminal law became more complicated all the time. It was more and more difficult for anyone to defend himself without a lawyer. And there was no reason to think that poor men charged with crimes needed lawyers any less than the rich.

The result of this trend was that the Supreme Court began to consider the problem of the poor man without a lawyer. The first great case was decided in 1932. It was called *Powell v. Alabama,* and it was a dramatic story.

The time was the middle of the Depression, when millions of Americans had no jobs and no money. On a freight car moving across Alabama were two groups of young people—nine Negro boys in one group, some white young men and girls in the other. They had a fight. At the village of Scottsboro, the Negroes were pulled off the train by a sheriff and accused of attacking the white girls. Local feeling against the Negroes was so violent that armed troops were sent in to keep order.

A few days later the Scottsboro Boys, as they came to be called, were put on trial for their lives. They had no lawyer. Their trials lasted just one day. The boys were found guilty and sentenced to death.

That was the case that reached the Supreme Court. The Court's opinion was a classic statement of the need for a lawyer. "Even the intelligent and educated man," the Court said, could not really defend himself against a criminal charge if he was not familiar with the law. "He lacks both the skill and knowledge adequately to prepare his defense, even though he have a perfect one. He requires the guiding hand of counsel at every step in the proceedings against him. Without it, though he be not guilty, he faces the danger of conviction because he does not know how to establish his innocence."

If all that was true of the educated man, the Court said in *Powell v. Alabama,* "how much more true is it of the ignorant and illiterate." Unanimously, the Supreme Court reversed the convictions of the Scottsboro Boys. It ruled that in their circumstances it had been "vital" to give them lawyers for their defense. Alabama had denied them due process of law.

It was a historic decision. For the first time the Supreme Court had found that the Constitution guaranteed free counsel for *some* poor, friendless defendants. But the Court had carefully not said that about *all* poor defendants. Its decision was limited to the extreme circumstances of the Scottsboro boys —helpless defendants surrounded by violent racial prejudice and facing death sentences.

Six years later, in 1938, the Supreme Court laid down a sweeping new rule for all *federal* criminal trials: Any defendant who could not afford a lawyer must have one free. There was no need, the Court ruled, for the defendant to show that he was ignorant or a victim of prejudice. If he was poor, the Sixth Amendment required that he be given a lawyer. The opinion was written by Justice Black.

There matters stood for four years. In *state* criminal trials, the Fourteenth Amendment required free lawyers for the poor in some cases, but not all. In *federal* courts, the Sixth Amendment demanded a lawyer for the poor in every case. Most people expected that the Supreme Court would soon apply the federal rule to the states so that lawyers would be required in both. But then, in 1942, came *Betts v. Brady*.

Smith Betts was a poor Maryland farmhand. He

was accused of robbery, and he asked the court to appoint a lawyer for him. The judge refused, explaining—just as the Florida judge was to tell Clarence Earl Gideon twenty years later—that he could appoint a lawyer only if Betts faced the death penalty. Betts, like Gideon, was convicted. The Supreme Court, by a vote of six to three, turned down Betts' claim that the conviction violated his right to a lawyer under the Fourteenth Amendment.

The Court's majority opinion examined the practice of all the states and found that they were divided about the necessity of appointing counsel for poor defendants. The Court concluded that most people did not consider the right to counsel "fundamental." It ruled that the right was therefore not guaranteed in all cases as a part of "due process of law." Moreover, the Court said, "the states should not be straitjacketed" in their handling of the criminal law. Betts had not shown that he was especially ignorant or that his case was complicated or that he suffered from some other "special circumstance," so he lost.

Justice Black dissented. No man should have to go to trial without a lawyer, he wrote, "merely because of his poverty. Any other practice seems to me to defeat the promise of our democratic society."

Within a few years the Supreme Court did make one change in the rule of *Betts v. Brady*. It made clear that when a poor man was charged with a capital crime—one that could bring the death sentence—he was always entitled to a lawyer. Otherwise, in *state* criminal cases, the Court continued to rule during the 1940's that the Constitution demanded counsel only in "special circumstances."

Then, after 1950, there was a swing away from *Betts v. Brady*. The case was criticized again and again in law reviews as unfair and illogical. And the Supreme Court seemed to be retreating quietly from its own decision, as it sometimes does. In case after case the Court found "special circumstances" that required counsel for a poor man. In effect the justices were paying lip service to *Betts v. Brady* but actually finding a need for a lawyer whenever a poor man succeeded in getting them to consider his case. And, even more significant, four justices announced that they were ready to overrule *Betts v. Brady* as soon as possible and make lawyers available to all poor men charged with serious crimes. One of them was, of course, Justice Black. With him were Chief Justice Earl Warren, Justice Douglas and Justice William J. Brennan Jr.

And apart from the issue of the right to counsel, the Supreme Court was moving in Justice Black's direction. The Court was showing less concern for the independence of the states and greater willingness to protect the individual. In a long series of cases, for example, it had set aside state criminal convictions because of the use of the "third degree"—torture and mental pressure to make prisoners confess.

In 1961, just a year before the Gideon case, the Court gave another notable sign of its new mood. Over the protest of Justice Frankfurter, it changed its mind about the use of illegally seized evidence in state criminal trials. The Court overruled its 1949 decision allowing such evidence. In a new case, *Mapp v. Ohio,* it held that the Fourth Amendment's prohibition on illegally seized material was "fundamental" and therefore applied to the states as part of "due process of law."

Mapp v. Ohio was most encouraging for the cause of Clarence Earl Gideon. The Supreme Court had been willing to overthrow a fairly recent decision and extend the protection of the individual despite the cry of "states' rights." Perhaps younger justices, grown up in a day when modern transportation and communications had brought the states so much closer together, cared less about our history of separate states and more about a single, American ideal of fairness in the law.

CHAPTER 6

The Brief for Gideon

WHEN Abe Fortas started to work on the Gideon case, he knew that his chances of winning were good. The Supreme Court seemed to be turning away from the old idea that the states should be allowed to do as they wished about criminal law. On the issue of the right to counsel, there were signs that the Court was coming to agree with the critics of *Betts v. Brady* and was ready now to enlarge the poor man's rights.

But this did not mean that there was nothing for

Fortas to do. The Supreme Court had picked a lawyer of unusual ability and experience to argue the case for Gideon. Clearly, the justices wanted to get from him the strongest possible arguments for taking the big step of making all fifty states provide lawyers for poor defendants. And each of the nine justices would have his own viewpoint. Fortas wanted to reach them all.

"It's hard for me to describe it without sounding stuffy," Fortas said later, discussing his own feelings. "A lawyer usually thinks about winning a case and doesn't care whether he wins by five-to-four or some other vote. But in this case—a constitutional case of fundamental importance, with all it meant for federal-state relations—it seemed to me that my duty was not just to try to win the case but to get as many justices as possible to go along with what I considered was the right result."

Fortas thought he had little chance of winning all nine justices' votes. He almost certainly started with four on his side, the four who had already come out for overruling *Betts v. Brady*—Justices Black, Brennan, Douglas and Warren. Another good possibility was Justice Tom C. Clark. He had often taken a tough line in criminal cases, opposing new protections for defendants, but he had written the Court's 1961 opinion in *Mapp v. Ohio*, making the states follow the federal rule against illegally seized evidence. Fortas was mildly hopeful about the two newest members of the Court, Justices Potter Stewart and Byron R. White, although they had not had much chance to indicate their views. He had little hope of persuading the two who most strongly supported independence for the states in criminal matters, Justice Frankfurter and Justice John Marshall Harlan.

When a court appoints a lawyer to represent someone, the lawyer's personal views about the rightness or wrongness of his poor client's case do not matter. His duty is to do his best for the client, like it or not.

But Fortas, as it happened, did personally agree that Clarence Earl Gideon should have had a lawyer when he was tried for breaking into the Bay Harbor Poolroom. He firmly believed that a criminal trial could not be fair unless there was a lawyer for the defense as well as one for the prosecution. Criminal law, he knew, had become more and more complicated in recent years. Along with new punishments there were new rights for the defendant, but they actually increased, not lessened, his need for a lawyer. How could he be expected to know, or insist to the judge on getting, his right to an unprejudiced jury, his right to keep out illegally seized evidence, his right to challenge a confession?

Fortas's own experience had persuaded him that a lawyer was essential to guide any defendant through the maze of a criminal trial. He wished there were some way to show the justices of the Supreme Court first-hand what it was like for a poor suspect down in some lowly criminal courtroom. He would like to have told the justices: "Let's not talk, let's go down and watch one of these fellows try to defend himself." But the business of persuading the Supreme Court is naturally more formal.

The first job ahead of Fortas was to write a *brief* —a printed statement of all the reasons he could think up for Clarence Earl Gideon to win his case. It would undoubtedly have to be quite a long piece of work, really a small book, going over all the legal debates about the right to counsel and the meaning of "due process of law" in the Fourteenth Amendment.

Fortas was not an expert on the Fourteenth Amendment in general or the right to counsel in particular, and so his first need was to educate himself. He began by calling in one of his partners in the law firm, Abe Krash, a younger man who had worked with him on some important cases before. He told Krash that he wanted to know everything there was to know about the right to counsel. The marvelous methods of a large law firm immediately started to work. What happens, in a good firm, is that bright young men look at a legal problem from every angle and write papers about every part of it. They use their imagination and try to cover all possible loopholes. Then more experienced lawyers take all this material and

81

weave it together. Their aim is to produce a brief that is not just a scattered collection of ideas but a concentrated, unified argument, going clearly from one point to the next and working up to a powerful conclusion.

The firm of Arnold, Fortas and Porter had taken on a Yale Law student that summer—John Hart Ely —who was there to get some practical experience before going back to Yale in the fall for his final year. Krash decided to have Ely do the main research, and for the next two months Ely worked on nothing but the Gideon case. A steady stream of typewritten memoranda went from him to Fortas and Krash, some in answer to questions they asked and some his own idea. His first was a list of recommended reading—thirty-two articles on *Betts v. Brady* that had appeared in various law reviews. Next he did a long memorandum going over in detail the history of what the Supreme Court had said about the Bill of Rights and the Fourteenth Amendment.

On July 25 Ely sent around the first paper really giving his own thoughts on the problem of counsel for poor criminal defendants. It was twenty-five pages long, and it was important.

Ely had taken a hard look at the way the theory of *Betts v. Brady*—that poor defendants should be given counsel when they suffer from "special circumstances"—actually worked. He had investigated how

82

it was applied in the state courts, especially the courts of Florida because Gideon's case came from there. He found that the state courts mentioned the same factors as the Supreme Court—circumstances such as feeble-mindedness that should entitle a defendant to counsel—but somehow came to different conclusions. They almost always rejected the poor men's requests for lawyers. Ely noted especially that the Supreme Court had reversed the Florida courts four times since 1959 for not finding "special circumstances" when they should have.

The confusion, Ely suggested, resulted from the fact that the Supreme Court had mentioned so many different reasons to be weighed in deciding whether counsel was essential in particular cases. He listed more than twenty that had been mentioned in majority or dissenting opinions in the Supreme Court. For example, justices had found a special need for counsel when the defendant was young or uneducated or stupid or faced a prejudiced prosecutor or an unfair judge. On the other hand, in deciding that defendants had not needed a lawyer, justices had mentioned such things as a helpful attitude on the part of the trial judge or the fact that the defendant had been through other trials and was experienced.

"It is difficult to imagine a case," Ely wrote, "in which at least five factors could not be listed on either side." He added that the Supreme Court did not stick to the same rules. In 1948 it had turned down a claim that a trial judge's mistake on a question of state law showed the need for a lawyer; that was not enough of a special circumstance, the majority said. But in 1961 the Court set aside a conviction because the judge had made just such a mistake about state law.

Then, in his memorandum, Ely explored an interesting idea. Maybe, he said, the rule of *Betts v. Brady* was so confusing that it produced the very kind of federal interference with state courts that it was supposed to avoid. State judges had to guess, from the vague list of "special circumstances," whether a poor man about to go on trial was entitled to a lawyer. If the Supreme Court decided later that they had guessed wrong, they had to try the man all over again. Moreover, Ely pointed out, a judge could scarcely even guess at the beginning of a trial whether the defendant was going to suffer some prejudice. He would probably never have seen the man before, and he could hardly start out by asking: "Are you stupid or sick or confused? If so, I'll have to appoint a lawyer for you."

Another weakness of the special-circumstances approach, Ely said, was that there was so little chance of correcting mistakes when judges made them. Thousands and thousands of poor men were convicted without lawyers in state courts every year, and very few even bothered to appeal. Ely said it was "unlikely that there are many convicts who, like Gideon, have the knowledge, ability and ambition to start an appeal."

The day after that long memorandum, July 26, Ely sent another one out. This one focused on the fact that, even under *Betts v. Brady*, the Supreme Court said counsel must always be given to poor men when they faced a capital charge. There was no constitutional reason to make a difference between capital cases and others, Ely said. The Fourteenth Amendment said the states could not take away a man's "life, *liberty* or *property* without due process of law." And the Supreme Court had just refused, in another area, to draw a line between capital and lesser charges. A law provided that civilians who go overseas with American soldiers—their wives, for example —should have military trials if they are accused of crimes. The Court found the law unconstitutional, ruling that civilians must have regular civilian trials. Justices Frankfurter and Harlan had wanted to restrict this ruling to cases in which civilians were accused of murder or other capital offenses, but Justice Clark for a majority of the Supreme Court said it must apply to all cases.

In another paper Ely urged Fortas not to repeat Justice Black's old argument that the Fourteenth Amendment was designed to "incorporate" the entire

Bill of Rights and apply it to the states. The Court had rejected that position, Ely said, and there was no use trying to revive it. Instead, Fortas should follow the line of argument that the right to counsel was so "fundamental" that it must be considered part of "due process of law" under the Fourteenth Amendment.

On August 3 Ely wrote a memorandum about Gideon's actual trial. He had studied the record of the trial to see whether the lack of a lawyer had hurt Gideon. At first glance, Ely wrote, the record seemed "to present the very model of the myth of *Betts v. Brady*: a case in which defense counsel is not needed." Gideon had shown skill in questioning the witnesses, Ely said, "and the judge went to great lengths to inform him of his rights." But a closer look convinced Ely that Gideon had not been able to defend himself very well. Ely pointed out several errors by the judge and examples of prejudice against Gideon.

"An argument could be made along the following lines," he wrote. "Here is a trial in which the defendant was skillful and the judge made every effort to protect his rights. Yet even here close examination of the law and of the facts reveals that defendant was repeatedly hurt by lack of counsel. If such unfairness happened in this trial, it would seem that there is *no* trial in which counsel is unnecessary. Thus the rule of *Betts v. Brady* is based upon a false factual assumption."

Here was a thought that caught the attention of Fortas. He combined it in his own mind with the idea that the special-circumstances approach might produce more, not less, interference with state courts. "I am convinced," Fortas explained later, "that this judge in Panama City, Florida, tried to help Gideon. He just did a bad job, as any judge would. It's not a judge's job to be a defense counsel. But how damaging it is for federal-state relations to have a federal court come along later and tell that judge that he did not do an adequate job!"

Fortas was more interested in practical questions, such as how the *Betts v. Brady* rule actually affected state courts, than he was in historical debates about the Fourteenth Amendment. Knowing the Supreme Court, he had the feeling that the justices would be most concerned about practical problems, too. For instance, some people warned gloomily that if the Court established the poor man's right to defense counsel in the Gideon case, the right would apply not only in serious cases like Gideon's but in trivial cases—even traffic offenses. If poor men demanded lawyers every time they got a parking ticket, these people said, there would not be enough lawyers in the whole country and our legal system would break down.

This forecast did not worry Fortas. He thought

very few men charged with traffic or other trivial offenses would want a lawyer—but if they did, he said, they ought to get one. But when he discussed this with Abe Krash, Krash said it would be unwise to risk scaring the Supreme Court by mentioning the possibility. Gideon had been charged with a *felony* (a serious crime) and given a five-year sentence. The Court therefore did not have to decide anything now except the right of a poor man to an appointed lawyer when he faced a serious charge.

An even more important practical question was what would happen, if Gideon won, to all the other men in prison who had been tried without a lawyer. Would the new rule requiring counsel be applied to them? Justice Frankfurter had warned years ago that a change in *Betts v. Brady* might have the effect of "opening wide the prison doors of the land."

But Fortas did not shrink from this fear either. For one thing, the Supreme Court did not have to decide in the Gideon case what it would do about men convicted without counsel in the past. And if a new rule were applied to past cases, the effect would not be to free all the prisoners who had not had a lawyer. They would simply have new trials, and whether they went free or were sent back to prison would depend on whether juries now found them guilty.

It was also true that most states now appointed

counsel for poor defendants in all serious criminal cases, although the Supreme Court had not said they were bound to do so by the Constitution. Prisoners in those states would therefore not be affected.

Exactly what was done in each state was not known until—in that same year, 1962—a law professor at the University of Minnesota, Yale Kamisar, decided to find out. Professor Kamisar discovered that thirty-seven states provided lawyers for the poor in all felony cases. In eight more states, most judges made it a practice to appoint counsel for poor felony defendants. That left only five states where the poor man was unlikely to have a lawyer for his defense unless he faced the death penalty—Alabama, Mississippi, North Carolina, South Carolina and Florida. Professor Kamisar, knowing about the Gideon case, telephoned Krash in September and asked whether he would like to see an advance copy of an article Kamisar had written about his findings. Krash said he would, and the copy arrived just in time to be used in writing the brief.

Ely went back to Yale Law School in September. Others in the office then took over the job of doing research assigned by Fortas or Krash. For example, Ralph Temple, a young associate in the firm, did essays on the right to counsel in England and on tne growth of American legal-aid plans—systems set up in some large cities to have lawyers always available in the courts for poor defendants.

Before leaving, Ely had written a proposed brief. Krash and Fortas liked it but wanted to make it stronger. Krash rewrote it into a second version. Then one weekend, on his way to join his wife in Westport, Connecticut, Fortas stopped at the Hotel Biltmore in New York and sat in a room for two days working out the kind of brief he wanted. From those notes on hotel stationery, and after a day's further talk with Fortas, Krash did a third draft. With some smoothing, it was the final version.

This description of how the brief was put together does not really indicate how much work went into it. Krash's office diary shows that in the last month of the brief's preparation he spent an average of six hours every day working on the case of Clarence Earl Gideon.

The brief was filed on November 21, 1962. It was fifty-three pages long, packing into that limited space many of the suggestions made in the memoranda from Ely and others.

An introductory section said the experience of lawyers and judges under the rule of *Betts v. Brady* had "not been a happy one. The quality of criminal justice and the relations between the federal and state courts have suffered." The idea of giving poor men lawyers only when they could show special need had not worked in practice to assure lawyers

where necessary. Nor had it meant any less interference with state courts. It would be less irritating
to state judges to follow a clear rule of counsel in
every serious criminal case than to have their decisions looked over, case by case, to see whether they
had done the right thing about counsel in light of
what happened at the trial.

That introduction reflected Fortas's deep feelings
about the case. Then the main part of the brief
made these major arguments:

First, the help of a lawyer is essential to "a fair
hearing" for a criminal defendant. Even a trained
lawyer will not handle his own defense; if he does,
the old saying goes, "he has a fool for his client."
The complete requirement of counsel in federal
courts, under the Sixth Amendment, shows that
people recognize the need for defense counsel. It
is wrong to count on the judge to protect the
defendant's rights, because a man cannot be both
judge and lawyer. And there is no good reason to
draw a line between criminal cases involving the
death penalty and others. The Fourteenth Amendment protects "liberty" and "property" as well as
"life," and the Court had rejected any distinction
in overseas trials of civilians connected with the
military.

Second, even those who believe most strongly in
federalism—the independence of the states—should

not favor the rule of *Betts v. Brady*. Professor Kamisar's study shows that most states now accept the idea of free lawyers for the poor in all serious criminal cases. The *Betts v. Brady* approach has caused tension between state and federal courts because it does not give "a clear-cut standard which state courts can follow." And a firm new rule requiring counsel would still leave plenty of room for experiments in the fifty states, because new ways would have to be found of providing the necessary lawyers.

Third, the idea of giving poor men lawyers only in "special circumstances" simply does not work in practice. The Supreme Court's own decisions about what those circumstances are have been confusing and contradictory. The state courts seldom find a need for counsel. Then poor prisoners have to work up their own appeals from the state decisions, and few of them are as determined as Gideon. Years may pass before the Supreme Court finds that a man should have had a lawyer at his trial, and that delay hurts both the man and the state.

Fourth, there are no practical reasons against adopting the rule that poor defendants must be given lawyers. If the decision does affect men already in prison, they would not go free but would be tried again. And in any event the states have had ample warning from the Supreme Court, in decisions ever since the case of the Scottsboro Boys thirty years ago, that the Court is deeply concerned about the right to counsel.

"For the reasons stated," the brief ended, *"Betts v. Brady* should be overruled, and the judgment of the court below should be reversed." The brief was signed by Fortas, Krash and Temple, and it noted the "valuable assistance" of one who could not sign because he was not yet a lawyer—"John Hart Ely, a third-year student at the Yale Law School, New Haven, Connecticut."

Fortas mailed the brief, as the Supreme Court's rules require, to the other side in the case—the Florida attorney general's office. He also sent a copy to Gideon in prison. Gideon answered on November 30, as follows:

Dear Sir:

This is to thank you for sending me a copy of the brief you have prepared and presented to the Supreme Court for my cause. Everyone and myself thinks it is a very wonderful and brilliant document.

I do not know how you have enticed the general public to take such an interest in this cause. But I must say it makes me feel very good.

Sincerely yours
Clarence Earl Gideon

CHAPTER 7

Gideon in Prison

GIDEON was an uneducated man, who had left school in the eighth grade and spent most of his life as a gambler and a thief and a prisoner. He could not have been expected to understand all the complicated arguments in Fortas's brief. And yet, somehow, he did understand—not all the details, perhaps, but the main idea. He knew that this was not just Clarence Earl Gideon's fight. He knew that his case had become an important part of a larger struggle to make all fifty American states live up to the ideals of the Constitution.

Or so it seemed to a stranger, interested in the case, who visited Gideon in the prison at Raiford, Florida.

"In Betts versus Brady," Gideon said, "the Supreme Court was trying to allow 'em their states' rights. It said the state courts could think things out for themselves, but they don't think. They just say no. They talk about states' rights. I think there's only one state—the United States."

It would be hard to imagine anyone who looked less as though he ought to be the subject of a great case in the Supreme Court of the United States. From the outside, Gideon seemed a man altogether defeated. He looked as though any hopes he had had for his life had long since burnt out—a used-up man who might have been fifteen years older than his actual age of fifty-two. His body was frail. He stood six feet tall, but a little stooped, and weighed only 140 pounds. His lower lip trembled, and he spoke in a slow, sad voice. In the prison file his card said: "Does not have anyone for the mailing or visiting list."

The scene of his supposed crime was just as miserable. Panama City was a town in the northwest panhandle of Florida, 1960 population 33,275. Twenty minutes out, on the outskirts of town, there was a giant plant of the International Paper Company, its tall chimneys pouring out thick yellow smoke. Huddled next to the factory fence, within sight and smell of the chemical smoke, was the village of Bay Harbor.

Village is too fancy a word for it. Bay Harbor looked like a frontier street in some old Western movie—after the street had been abandoned and allowed to gather dust for years. Bay Harbor was made up of just a few decaying buildings separated by dirt roads and alleys and empty yards filled with weeds. There were a bar, a grocery, a two-story building labeled "Hotel"—and the Bay Harbor Poolroom that Gideon was accused of breaking into.

By comparison, the state prison where Gideon now made his temporary home, about 200 miles east, was cheerful. Inside a strong steel fence were small buildings, green lawns and beautifully kept flowers and shrubs. "Trusties"—prisoners trusted to behave —wore white coats and trousers like hospital assistants' and were allowed to wander around freely. During the lunch hour some of them sat around outside in the sun, smoking pipes and reading.

Gideon was a trusty. The visitor was brought to meet him in what the prisoners called "the courtroom," an empty room with a long table that they used when they wrote to courts, trying to get out. There were no law books, and Gideon began the conversation by complaining about that.

"Here's the place where you have to write your petition," he said, "and you don't have any help. That's what hurts you. The Supreme Court sent me a book of rules, but I can't understand that. The rules take a pretty educated man to understand them."

Still, Gideon had done pretty well without help in writing his petition to the Supreme Court. He had persuaded the Court to hear his case out of hundreds. And it was clear that Gideon now saw himself as prison legal expert and enjoyed that position.

"There's no real lawyers in here now," he said. "I guess I know more than most, and I help out. I have one boy in here that can't read or write. I wrote a letter to the Supreme Court of Florida for him asking them to appoint an attorney to write him a petition. They took that letter as a petition and turned it down without a hearing, so I wrote the whole thing over and sent it to the Supreme Court of the U.S." (This prisoner's name was Allen Baxley Jr. The Supreme Court, it turned out, was waiting to act on his case until after it had decided Gideon's.)

Gideon rolled his own cigarettes. He tapped the tobacco into a cigarette paper and rolled it in his long, rather artistic fingers, stained yellow from all the tobacco they had handled. Then he paid a compliment to Abe Fortas. "I notice he never makes a statement that isn't well thought out," Gideon said. "He never writes you anything that isn't exactly that way."

It appeared that Gideon had also been exactly right in what he had written to Fortas in that long letter about his life. The prison records showed the same crimes that he had listed:

1928, burglary in Missouri, 10-year sentence, paroled after 3 years.

1934, theft of property from a federal armory, 3 years.

1940, another Missouri burglary, 10-year sentence, escaped in 1944, recaptured in 1945, released in 1950.

1951, burglary in Texas, 2 years, released in 1952.

After that there was nothing serious in the record until the charge about the Bay Harbor Poolroom in June, 1961. The papers did show that Gideon had previously been arrested as a drunk in Panama City and spent a few days in jail for that.

The prison officers did not seem to mind Gideon's activities in the law. One said: "Usually when prisoners are trying to get out legally, you know they behave perfectly around here." The warden and his assistants knew all about Gideon's case, but the possibility that he might win and even help other prisoners who had been convicted without a lawyer did not seem to bother them. An assistant warden said: "Our feeling is: boys, if you can get out of here legal, we're with you."

The visitor asked Gideon why he had insisted so firmly on a lawyer, all the way from that courtroom in Panama City to the Supreme Court of the United States.

"I knew that was my only chance," he said. "I don't know if you've ever been in a courtroom in one of these small Florida towns, but they're prejudiced. They just run over people who have nothing. I've never taken the witness stand in this case, nobody knows what I'd say. Without a lawyer, with the criminal record I had, whatever I'd say they'd never have paid any attention to."

The idea that Florida officials were against the poor was fixed in Gideon's mind. He complained that they were trying to take his children away from him and put them out for adoption while he was in prison. As men in jail often do, Gideon complained of so many raw deals that he was soon hard to believe. Sometimes, in fact, his bitter comments wandered, and he had to be steered back to the point. But he never made any effort to paint his own life as good. He only wanted his rights.

"You can't justify a crime," he said, "whether it's murder or the smallest burglary. But they can go by the book in trying you and sentencing you."

On one thing his mind was very clear—his respect

for the United States Supreme Court. It was up to that Court, he said, to make sure that poor men everywhere had lawyers for their defense. "Without the Supreme Court it might have happened some time," he said. "But it wouldn't have happened in this state soon."

He would not come right out and say so, but there was every sign that he expected the Supreme Court to rule in his favor. He said all the prisoners were thinking about the case, "even though the intelligence of the people in here is not the greatest in the world." A lot of the men, he said, "think they're just going to have to bring buses in here and turn 'em loose."

That was a little too confident. The State of Florida still had its chance to persuade the Supreme Court that it should be allowed to go on handling Gideon's case, and others like it, as before.

CHAPTER 8
The Other Briefs

IN the ordinary criminal case the balance of power favors the state. It has vastly more men and money to use in the case than the defendant it is prosecuting. Certainly that had been true at the trial of Clarence Earl Gideon. But now, in the Supreme Court, the balance was suddenly the other way.

A large and expert Washington law firm had spent hundreds and hundreds of hours working for Gideon. On the other side, trying to keep Gideon in prison, there was one young lawyer who had never set foot in the Supreme Court. He was Bruce Robert Jacob, an assistant attorney general of Florida, twenty-six years old when the case started its way through the Supreme Court.

Bruce Jacob was a tall, blond, serious-looking young man whose life reached all sorts of turning points during the Gideon case. In the middle of his work on the case, he left the state attorney general's office to join a private law firm. He also won a commission as a second lieutenant in the National Guard, and he was married. It was a busy year.

Jacob was born March 26, 1935, in Chicago, and moved to Florida with his family when he was in junior high school. He went to Principia, a Christian Science college in Illinois, but finished at Florida State University and then Stetson Law School in St. Petersburg, Florida. He had been working in the state attorney general's office for two years when the Gideon case came along and was assigned to him. The attorney general of Florida, Richard W. Ervin, was formally in charge and signed the papers. But Jacob wrote most of them, appeared before the Supreme Court on his own and was responsible for the case from beginning to end.

He learned that the Supreme Court had agreed to hear Gideon's claim when he read a newspaper story in June, 1962. A letter from the Court arrived a few days later. Jacob was due to leave just then for two weeks at a National Guard training school. Before he left, he discussed the case with one of the older men in the office, George Georgieff. Georgieff suggested that Jacob arrange to have Florida send a letter to the other forty-nine states asking them to join in the case, on Florida's side, by filing *amicus curiae* briefs. *Amicus curiae* is Latin for "friend of the court." It refers to someone who is not personally involved in a lawsuit but who gives his views to the court because he has some experience or interest in the problem that the actual parties are debating. For example, when the issue of school segregation was tested in the Supreme Court, various Southern states filed *amicus curiae* briefs urging the Court to allow segregation. The American Civil Liberties Union—a private organization that fights for the rights of individuals—and other groups filed briefs on the opposite side.

The night before he left for National Guard camp, Jacob wrote the letter to the states. Attorney General Ervin approved it and sent it out to the forty-nine other state attorneys general.

The letter first stated that the Supreme Court had agreed to hear the Gideon case and to take a fresh look at the question of poor criminal defendants' right to counsel. Four justices, the letter noted, had already urged the Court to overrule the 20-year-old case of *Betts v. Brady* and say that all poor men facing serious criminal charges must be given lawyers. If the four could get just one more vote, the letter warned, "*Betts v. Brady* will be overruled and the states will be required to appoint counsel in all felony cases. Such a decision would infringe on [interfere with] the right of the states to determine their own rules of criminal procedure."

Having given that dramatic warning, the letter asked all the other states to help Florida defend *Betts v. Brady* and states' rights. It urged them to file *amicus curiae* briefs and to send any helpful information or suggestions to the Florida attorney general's office.

The idea behind the letter seemed quite a clever one. State attorneys general often file *amicus curiae* briefs in the Supreme Court, and their purpose is almost always to resist some proposal that they view as an interference with the independence of the states. When the Supreme Court was considering whether it was constitutional for New York schools to begin each day with a special prayer in class, twenty-two states filed a brief asking that New York be allowed to continue the prayer. Now the Gideon case presented, as Jacob saw it, a much more dangerous threat to states' rights. Anyone would have expected many states to reply enthusiastically to Florida's letter and to file briefs on its side. What actually happened was astonishingly different.

In the middle of August, two months after Jacob's letter went out, a reply came in from the attorney general of Minnesota, Walter F. Mondale. "I believe in states' rights too," Mondale wrote, "but I also believe in the Bill of Rights. Nobody knows better than an attorney general or prosecuting attorney that rules of criminal law which baffle trained professionals can only overwhelm the [ignorant]. . . . Since I firmly believe that any person charged with a felony should [have] counsel regardless of his financial condition, I would welcome a requirement that counsel be appointed in all state felony prosecutions."

Mondale's letter annoyed Jacob. "I thought everyone should have a lawyer, we all thought that," he said later. "But I thought the states should do it by themselves, not have it imposed on them by the Supreme Court." Jacob also felt Mondale did not fully understand that it was the job of the Florida attorney general's office, whatever the personal beliefs of the men there, to present the other side of the Gideon case to the Supreme Court, because the Court always wants to hear both sides. Jacob therefore wrote Mondale an answering letter that was signed by Attorney General Ervin. "As I see it," the letter said, "my duty is to present to the Supreme Court the strongest possible argument [for sticking to] *Betts v. Brady.* My personal feelings on whether *Betts* is a good rule do not matter."

Mondale sent copies of this exchange of letters to another state attorney general whom he knew, Edward J. McCormack Jr. of Massachusetts. McCormack gave them to an assistant who was concerned especially about the rights of poor and unfortunate men, Gerald A. Berlin. Some time later, when Berlin was vacationing on Martha's Vineyard, he talked with some friends about Florida's request for help in the Gideon case and Mondale's answer. At that point the thought came to him of writing an *amicus curiae* brief on the opposite side from Florida —on Gideon's side. Quickly Berlin got the approval of his chief, McCormack. With the help of some professors at the Harvard Law School, Berlin wrote the brief.

Massachusetts, then, was going to support Gideon's claim. But Berlin and McCormack were not satisfied with that; they wanted other states to join them. They telephoned Mondale in Minnesota and won his quick agreement. Then all three of them set out to persuade the attorneys general of other states by letter and telephone. Under the rules of the Supreme Court the brief had to be filed at about the same time as that of the side it was supporting. It arrived at the Supreme Court on November 23, just two days after Fortas's brief. By then Berlin, McCormack and Mondale had won the support of twenty-three states. They were Massachusetts, Minnesota, Alaska, Colorado, Connecticut, Georgia, Hawaii, Idaho, Illinois, Iowa, Kentucky, Maine, Michigan, Missouri, Nevada, New Jersey, North Dakota, Ohio, Oregon, Rhode Island, South Dakota, Washington and West Virginia.

It was an astonishing event in the Supreme Court's history to have twenty-three states file a brief asking the Court to make them obey a new constitutional rule. Three of the states that signed—Hawaii, Maine and Rhode Island—did not even have any regular system for providing lawyers to poor defendants in serious criminal cases, and they would therefore have to make immediate changes if the Court ruled in Gideon's favor. And the others might have to improve their systems. When one member of the Supreme Court saw this *amicus curiae* brief, he said he would not have been surprised if the Court instead had received a brief from forty-nine states supporting Florida's position. Fortas was just as astounded as the justices. He knew nothing about the Massachusetts-Minnesota effort until he got a copy of the brief in the mail.

The brief for the twenty-three states made many of the same arguments as Fortas. Berlin, in the brief, said the theory of *Betts v. Brady*—that poor defendants must show "special circumstances" to obtain lawyers—was a "curious" one. Supreme Court justices had constantly disagreed on what it meant, he said, so it was "unrealistic" to expect other judges to under-

107

stand when they were supposed to appoint lawyers. *Betts v. Brady*, the brief concluded, had produced "twenty years of bad law. That in the world of today a man may be condemned to [prison] for lack of means to supply counsel for his defense is unthinkable."

Another *amicus curiae* brief was filed on Gideon's side by the American Civil Liberties Union. It was signed by J. Lee Rankin, a distinguished former lawyer for the federal government, now in private practice in New York. This brief included an interesting look at the way state courts had handled questions about the right to counsel under the rule of *Betts v. Brady*. In forty-four cases, for example, the higher courts of Pennsylvania had written opinions on whether a prisoner should have had a lawyer at his trial. In only one did these Pennsylvania judges find that the defendant had been wrongly denied counsel. In Maryland the higher courts found only three cases out of thirty-eight in which a prisoner should have been given a lawyer. The Civil Liberties Union brief concluded that state courts very rarely found the "special circumstances" needed for a lawyer under *Betts v. Brady*. It urged the Supreme Court to drop that approach.

There was also one *amicus curiae* brief on Florida's side, asking the Supreme Court to stick to the rule of *Betts v. Brady*. This was filed by two states, Alabama and North Carolina—the only two, in the end, that responded favorably to Florida's letter asking for help. This brief was written by George D. Mentz, an assistant attorney general of Alabama who had argued one case on the right to counsel in the Supreme Court. It made a strong appeal to let the states have their independence, especially in dealing with crime.

Some day, Mentz's brief said, poor defendants might all have lawyers and poor men all the food and clothes and other "creature comforts" they wanted. That was a fine ideal that Americans might aim for, but it was not required by the Fourteenth Amendment or any other part of the Constitution. Progress should come from the people themselves, not through some command from the Supreme Court.

Mentz's brief then turned to some practical problems. Farm and country areas, he said, sometimes had very few lawyers. There might be "more persons charged with crime" than lawyers who knew anything about criminal cases. (Most American lawyers handle only civil cases, which are mostly disputes between private individuals or companies about money or property.) As a matter of fact, Mentz said, a poor man had a better chance of getting a jury to treat him kindly without a lawyer than with one, especially if the lawyer was not experienced in criminal cases.

Even if the approach of *Betts v. Brady* had gone

109

wrong occasionally, Mentz concluded, it remained "the best one for our American way of life." Any decision to require counsel for all poor men "charged with crime in state courts should come not from this [Supreme] Court but from the people of the individual states acting through their elected legislatures or judges."

That left only Florida's brief to be filed. Jacob had expected to finish it during the summer, but too many other things kept happening. He and a girl who worked near him in the State Capitol building, Ann Wear, decided to get married. He also accepted an invitation from a law firm in Bartow, Florida, to go to work for them, and he and Ann had to move to Bartow by October. They were married on September 8, had a week's honeymoon on the island of Jamaica and then set up their new household in Bartow.

By the time he got to work on his brief, in the fall, Jacob had lost just about all hope of winning the Gideon case. The fact that twenty-three states had filed a brief against him was a bad sign. But the most discouraging blow had been the news, on August 29, that Justice Frankfurter had retired from the Court because of ill health. More than any member of the Supreme Court, Justice Frankfurter respected this country's history of separate states and wanted to allow the states independence from the central, federal government. Not only his vote on the Court, but his leadership, seemed to Jacob essential if there was to be any chance of preserving the rule of *Betts v. Brady*. To take Justice Frankfurter's place, President Kennedy named the Secretary of Labor, Arthur J. Goldberg, a younger man who had grown up in different times and could not be expected to have the same ideas as Justice Frankfurter about the states.

"I had been developing some hope," Jacob said later, "that the Court would draw back" from the big step of overturning *Betts v. Brady*. "But when Justice Frankfurter retired, I realized that we had very little chance."

But lawyers have to do their job whether they expect to win or not. Jacob had obtained permission from Attorney General Ervin of Florida to carry on with the Gideon case after he resigned as assistant attorney general and moved to Bartow. It was hard, though, to find time to work on the case while he was trying to catch on to his new job in the law firm. What he did was to worry about the Gideon case on nights and weekends. Because there was no good law library in Bartow, Jacob and his wife drove 250 miles to the State Capitol in Tallahassee nearly every weekend to use the library of the Florida Supreme Court. He would read books and point out what he thought were important sections; then Ann would copy those down. Finally, in late November, he wrote the brief out in longhand at home, and Ann typed it up. There

111

could hardly have been a more striking contrast to the time and help available in Abe Fortas's law firm in the preparation of the brief for Gideon.

Jacob's brief began with a section arguing that, if *Betts v. Brady* was still good law, Gideon had not suffered from any "special circumstances" and so did not need a lawyer. He said the record of Gideon's trial showed that he had "much skill in questioning witnesses." Moreover, Jacob argued, Gideon had been convicted of four serious crimes before this one and so had some experience in courtrooms. Jacob had also got a letter on this point from the judge who had been in charge of the original trial, Robert L. McCrary Jr. The letter was not quoted in the brief, but Jacob sent it along separately to the Supreme Court. Judge McCrary said his opinion was that "Gideon had both the mental capacity and the experience in the courtroom to adequately conduct his defense. . . . In my opinion he did as well as most lawyers could have done in handling his case."

Next, in his brief, Jacob made his main argument —that the Supreme Court should not make any change in the rule of *Betts v. Brady*.

Our whole system of government, Jacob wrote, is against the idea of tying the states to one national rule on how to handle criminal cases. For the Supreme Court to announce a fixed, unchangeable rule requiring counsel for the poor would "defeat the very

112

desirable possibility of state experiment in the field of criminal procedure." Moreover, the present system of requiring counsel only when prisoners could show a special need was a fair reflection of the "due process of law" demanded by the Fourteenth Amendment, since that was a deliberately vague phrase, not a specific set of regulations.

Jacob denied that the Court had made it hard for the states to understand what it meant by "special circumstances" under *Betts v. Brady.* The various cases explaining that rule were "clear and consistent," Jacob said, and lawyers were used to having the law worked out case by case.

Then Jacob warned that there could be grave results if the justices made state courts follow the same requirements for giving lawyers to the poor that federal courts had to apply under the Sixth Amendment. The line could not really be drawn at serious criminal charges. Lawyers would sooner or later be required in lesser cases, too, and there would be "an enormous burden" on lawyers. More defendants who used to plead guilty would want to fight their cases, so courts would be busier and there would be "unnecessary expense to the taxpayer."

Most serious of all, Jacob said, was the possibility of what a victory for Gideon might mean to men already in prison. He said he had asked to have a survey made of the Florida prisons. It showed that of the

7,836 men then in those prisons, 5,093 had had no lawyers when they were tried. "If *Betts v. Brady* should be overruled by this Court," Jacob said, "as many as 5,093 hardened criminals" might get out "in Florida alone, not to mention those in other states." At the very least, he urged, if the Court decided this case in favor of Gideon, it should make clear that the decision did not affect anyone already in jail.

The brief for the state of Florida was filed soon after Christmas. Jacob still had one big job to do in the Gideon case—to appear before the Supreme Court and argue the case in person. Even before the brief was filed, he had a letter from the office of the Court's clerk telling him that the case would be "reached for argument on Monday, January 14, 1963."

CHAPTER 9

Argument
Before the Court

ONE of the most fascinating scenes in Washington is the argument of a case before the Supreme Court. Even the visitor unfamiliar with law can get a good sense of how the Court works by sitting in the back of the courtroom and listening. There are the lawyers for each side in a case, on their feet one at a time, telling the justices why they ought to win and then answering the questions that come flying at them. The thorough discussion of a single case, if it is done well, shows how our system of law tries to find

115

the truth in the clash of opposing views. It also shows how difficult the questions are that the Supreme Court has to decide. Typically, the listener finds himself persuaded by the last voice he has heard.

Oral argument—oral meaning by mouth, in contrast to the lawyers' written argument in briefs—is more important to the Court than many lawyers realize. Too often lawyers think it is just a ceremony, an old-fashioned business that does not really matter as long as all the arguments are in the brief. The justices do not feel that way. A good oral argument, Justice Harlan has said, "may in many cases make the difference between winning and losing, no matter how good the briefs are."

There are two reasons why oral argument matters so much to the Court. One is that a brief cannot answer back when a justice reading it thinks of a question. During oral argument a question from the Court gives the lawyer a great opportunity to settle doubts and solve problems that the justices see in the case. The second reason is that argument comes at a crucial time—just before the nine justices take their first vote on a case. Arguments are held Monday through Thursday, and then on Friday the justices at their conference ordinarily vote on all the cases that have been heard that week. The oral arguments are likely to be fresh in their minds.

Considering how important oral arguments can be,

it is sad to say that most of them are badly done. Lawyers appearing before the Supreme Court are frequently nervous, unprepared or, worst of all, over-confident. One mistake they make is to dodge questions so that they can stick to an argument they have written out ahead of time. The justices want their questions answered and would much rather have a lawyer talk to them informally than read to them from a script. Another mistake is to lecture the Court on high-sounding ideas without ever mentioning the facts of the particular case. That tends to make the justices look sleepy. They like it when a lawyer tells them the facts in a simple, direct way. Often, in their questions, they try to find out what a case means to the human beings involved. It is almost as if the justices—alone in their marble building, trying to solve such big problems—wanted to be reminded of the real world of men and women outside.

One of the hardest things for lawyers who appear before the Supreme Court for the first time is fitting everything they have to say into a limited time. The Court limits most arguments to either one or two hours, divided evenly between the opposite sides. In the Gideon case Abe Fortas and Bruce Jacob each had an hour. In addition, quite unusually, the Court had allowed half an hour for argument by a friend of the court on each side—Lee Rankin of the American

Civil Liberties Union for Gideon, Assistant Attorney General George Mentz of Alabama for the State of Florida.

The oral argument was nothing new to Fortas, who had appeared in the Supreme Court many times before. But Bruce Jacob, who had never even seen the courtroom in that great white building, looked forward to it with much uneasiness. Jacob flew to Washington on Saturday, January 12, 1963, two days before he had been told the Gideon case would come up for argument. The flight was bumpy, doing nothing to improve his already unsettled stomach. He spent the weekend in his hotel, worrying over what questions he might be asked, worrying in general.

As he walked into the Supreme Court building that Monday morning and then for the first time saw the justices at work, Jacob felt the confusing contrast that anyone with a sharp eye should notice there. For the Supreme Court is a place of curious contrasts— at the same time large and small, full of ceremony and yet the most informal and approachable branch of the government.

The building is grand in size—a "great marble temple," one guidebook says, whose "mighty splendor" seems to have little to do with the actual business of government. The visitor who walks up the marble steps and past the huge marble columns on the outside finds himself in a long, cold hall, again all marble. Bronze gates keep him out of the back half of the building, where the justices work in private in their offices, library and conference room. The courtroom, which is open to the public, strengthens the visitor's sense of being in a temple. There are more columns, an enormously high ceiling and a carved frieze of the great legal men of history way up on the marble walls. The Marshal of the Court smashes his gavel down on a wooden block, everyone stands up and the justices file in through the red velvet curtains behind the bench as the Marshal sounds the traditional cry: "The honorable, the Chief Justice and the Associate Justices of the Supreme Court of the United States. Oyez, oyez, oyez. All persons having business before the honorable, the Supreme Court of the United States, are admonished to draw near and give their attention, for the Court is now sitting. God save the United States and this honorable Court."

But then, when an argument begins, the awesome sense of being in a temple fades away. The scene becomes extraordinarily informal, and the room suddenly seems small. The justices and the lawyers talk, and it is just that—good talk, without frills, direct and friendly and sometimes even funny.

"It was nothing like I expected," Bruce Jacob said later. "It was so informal—I just couldn't believe it. Usually judges are so sober-looking; they don't laugh.

Not that they're inhuman, but they're nothing like Supreme Court justices. I just got the impression that these men had a real good time, talking to each other and asking questions."

The Gideon case had a new number on the Court's calendar, 155. It was not reached for argument that Monday, January fourteenth. The clerk's office always has lawyers come to the courtroom ahead of time, so that there is no chance that one argument will be finished before the next one is ready for the justices. No exact time is set for a case to start. The Court hears argument from 10 A.M. to 2:30 P.M., with half an hour out for lunch from 12 to 12:30, and when one case is finished the next one is called.

On that Monday the justices first read some of their opinions in cases that had been argued earlier in the term. Then argument of another case began. At noon there was an interruption because this happened to be the day of the President's State of the Union message. The justices went over to the Capitol, which is just a few hundred yards away, to hear President Kennedy. Later that afternoon and the next morning the lawyers in the Gideon case sat in the courtroom listening to other cases being argued. At 11:06 on Tuesday morning it was their turn.

Chief Justice Warren, as is his custom, announced the next case by reading its full title aloud: "Number 155, Clarence Earl Gideon, petitioner, versus H. G.

Cochran Jr., director, Division of Corrections, State of Florida." From his desk, at the left of the raised bench on which the justices sit, Clerk of the Court John Davis said: "Counsel are present." The lawyers in the Gideon case moved forward to two long tables just below the bench.

The justices were seated in an order fixed by tradition. At the far right, as the audience saw them, was the newest member of the Court, Arthur J. Goldberg of Illinois, fifty-four years old, gray-haired, who had been an outstanding labor lawyer before serving as Secretary of Labor. At the far left was President Kennedy's other appointee, Byron R. White of Colorado, forty-five, a one-time All-America football player and also a Rhodes Scholar, who still appeared both strong and scholarly. Next to Justice Goldberg was Potter Stewart of Ohio, forty-seven, looking almost young enough to be still at college, appointed by President Eisenhower in 1958. Second from the left was the small, bouncy figure of William J. Brennan Jr., fifty-six, a judge of the New Jersey Supreme Court when he was picked by Eisenhower in 1956. Again to the right was John Marshall Harlan, sixty-three, a noted New York lawyer named by Eisenhower in 1955, looking perhaps more like a judge than anyone else—and rightly so because his grandfather, of the same name, had been a Supreme Court justice. Third from the left was Tom C. Clark, sixty-

121

three, a friendly Texan, former Attorney General, the only appointee of President Truman (1949) still on the Court. To the right of the Chief Justice was William O. Douglas, sixty-four, a ruddy-faced out-doorsman from the State of Washington, law school professor and government official named by President Roosevelt in 1939. To the left of the Chief was Hugo L. Black, seventy-six years old but still a tough tennis player, a Senator from Alabama when Roosevelt put him on the Court in 1937. Finally, at the center sat Earl Warren, seventy-one, the popular governor of California for ten years, Republican candidate for Vice President in 1948, a huge white-haired man named Chief Justice by Eisenhower in 1953.

The lawyer arguing a case stands at a small desk between the two counsel tables, facing the Chief Justice. The side that lost in the lower courts and is asking the Supreme Court to reverse their decision goes first; so the argument in the Gideon case was begun by Abe Fortas. As he stood up, the Chief Justice gave him the usual greeting: "Mr. Fortas." And he made the usual opening: "Mr. Chief Justice, may it please the Court . . ."

Fortas began telling the justices the facts of the case. In his deep, almost mournful voice, occasionally taking off his horn-rimmed glasses and waving them, he told about the morning Clarence Earl Gideon was supposed to have broken into the Bay Harbor Poolroom and stolen "some wine, perhaps some cigarettes and an unstated amount of money." Fortas described how Gideon took part in his own trial, tried to cross-examine the witnesses, talked to the jury. Then, on this foundation of the facts, Fortas started to build his legal argument.

"This record does not indicate that Clarence Earl Gideon was a person of low intelligence," Fortas said, "or that the judge was unfair to him. But to me this case shows the basic difficulty with Betts against Brady. It shows that no man, however intelligent, can conduct his own defense well."

At that point Justice Harlan broke in. He was now, after the retirement of his friend Justice Frankfurter, the Court's strongest believer in federalism. Fortas expected to have the hardest time persuading him to overrule *Betts v. Brady*.

"That's not the point, is it, Mr. Fortas?" Justice Harlan asked. "*Betts* didn't go on the assumption that a man can do as well without an attorney as he can with one, did it? Everyone knows that isn't so."

As a matter of fact, Justice Harlan was not correct. The opinion in *Betts v. Brady* had suggested that in a simple case a lawyer was not even needed. Bruce Jacob was prepared to argue that Gideon did just as well without a lawyer.

But Fortas did not indicate disagreement with Justice Harlan. Instead he shrewdly accepted the

123

statement as a help to his side and argued on from it.

"I entirely agree, Mr. Justice Harlan, with the point you are making: namely, that of course a man cannot have a fair trial without a lawyer, but *Betts* held that this was outweighed by the demands of federalism. . . .

"How can our civilized nation pretend," Fortas went on, "that there is a fair trial without the counsel for the prosecution doing all he can within the limits of decency, and the counsel for the defense doing his best within the same limits, and from that clash will emerge the truth? . . . I think there is a tendency to forget what happens to these poor, miserable people in the strange and awesome surroundings of a criminal court. . . .

"And so the real basis of Betts against Brady must be the understanding sensitivity of this Court to the pull of federalism."

This last statement of Fortas's about "understanding sensitivity" seemed to anger Justice Harlan. It was not clear why, because all Fortas had meant was that the Court in *Betts v. Brady* had thought the need for a lawyer was outbalanced by the wisdom of leaving the states alone. Justice Harlan, usually such a gentle man, turned red, leaned forward and said quite sharply: "Really, Mr. Fortas, 'understanding sensitivity' seems to me a most unfortunate term to describe one of the fundamental principles of our constitutional system."

"Mr. Justice Harlan," Fortas replied without a flicker of nervousness, "I believe in federalism. But I believe that Betts against Brady does not show a proper regard for federalism. It requires a case-by-case supervision by this Court of state criminal proceedings, and that cannot be wholesome. . . . Intervention should be in the least abrasive [irritating] way possible."

That was the argument that Fortas considered central to his case. He had expected to make it later, after more of a build-up, but Justice Harlan's question had given him the chance to make the point dramatically. As a skillful lawyer he had put aside his prepared plans and made the thrust at once. Whether the answer satisfied Justice Harlan only the justice knew, but he did lean back and look somewhat happier.

Fortas traced the history of the right-to-counsel cases decided by the Supreme Court, from the Scottsboro case in 1932 through *Betts v. Brady* in 1942 and on up to the present. He criticized the *Betts* formula of "special circumstances" as impossible to understand clearly. There were more questions.

JUSTICE STEWART: "When was the last time we did *not* find special circumstances in a case here? I think there have been none since I came on the Court."

FORTAS: "I think it was the case of Quicksall against Michigan, in 1950. . . . This approach is wrong. How can a judge, when a man is brought before him, look at him and say there are special circumstances? Does the judge look at him and say: 'You look stupid'? It is unworkable."

JUSTICE HARLAN: "The states are recognizing that."

Fortas again agreed with Justice Harlan. Most states now did provide lawyers for poor defendants in all serious cases. Fortas mentioned the findings of Professor Kamisar. But the fact that the states were moving to provide counsel, he said, was an argument *for* regarding a lawyer's help as a constitutional right under the Fourteenth Amendment—because it showed that most people now did consider the right to a lawyer "fundamental." He noted especially the brief filed by twenty-three states in favor of overruling *Betts v. Brady* and said he was "proud of this document as an American."

"We may be comforted in this constitutional moment," Fortas said, "by the fact that what we are doing is a deliberate change after twenty years of experience—a change that has the overwhelming support of the bench [judges], the bar [lawyers] and even the states."

It was noon, and the justices rose for lunch. Afterward Fortas hoped to say just a few words more, then save about ten minutes for a reply after Jacob spoke, as the opening side is allowed to do. But the justices were still throwing questions at him when the

126

Marshal of the Court, sitting to the right of the bench, switched on a small white light to show him that he had only five minutes left.

Justice Stewart asked whether he was right in gathering that Fortas was not going to make the old argument that the Fourteenth Amendment had been intended to "incorporate" the entire Bill of Rights and apply it to the states. Fortas agreed—he was not. But the answer that pleases one justice may bother another. This one bothered the member of the Court who had fought so long for the idea that the Bill of Rights should be considered incorporated in the Fourteenth Amendment—Justice Black. He asked in a puzzled way why Fortas was not making that argument.

"Mr. Justice Black," Fortas replied, "I like that argument that you have made so eloquently. But I cannot as an advocate [lawyer] make that argument because this Court has rejected it so many times. I hope you never stop making it."

There was laughter in the courtroom, and Justice Black joined in.

A red light went on in front of Fortas, meaning that his hour was up. But as he sat down, Chief Justice Warren gave him an additional five minutes to reply after Jacob, adding the same to Jacob's time.

Next came Lee Rankin, arguing for the American Civil Liberties Union on Gideon's side. His voice

127

was soft, his words sincere. He spoke less about this particular case and more about the whole American system of law.

"Judges have a special responsibility here," Rankin said "and so do lawyers. It just isn't true that laymen [non-lawyers] know these rules of law [the complicated rules of criminal trials]. That's what's wrong with Betts against Brady. It's time—long past time—that our legal profession stood up and said: 'We know a man cannot get a fair trial when he defends himself.'"

At 1:10 in the afternoon Bruce Jacob's turn came. He stood up looking extremely young and earnest. He had hardly begun talking when the questions poured down at him. Through his whole argument he had scarcely one five-minute period when he could talk without interruption. Considering how difficult his case was and how new the whole business of arguing to the Supreme Court was for him, he stood up bravely.

JUSTICE BLACK: "Why isn't Betts against Brady as much of an interference with the states as a flat rule requiring counsel? One of my reactions to *Betts* was the uncertainty in which it leaves the states."

JACOB: "I don't think *Betts* is that unclear."

JUSTICE BLACK: "How do you know what the 'special circumstances' are?"

JACOB: "Each time this Court decides a case, we know another special circumstance."

JUSTICE BRENNAN: "In recent years—in four cases I think—we have reversed cases from your state every time."

JACOB: "We [still] prefer case-by-case decision. . . . It may not be precise, but we prefer it because it gives the state some freedom in making its own rules of criminal procedure."

* * *

JUSTICE BLACK: "What historical support have you found for the distinction between capital and non-capital cases?"

JACOB: "Your Honor, I can't think of any."

JUSTICE BLACK: "I can't either. That's why I asked."

JACOB: "There is a practical distinction between capital and noncapital cases if you want to draw the line somewhere. Everyone is fearful of being put to death."

JUSTICE BLACK: "Maybe they're fearful of spending years in prison, too."

Jacob talked finally about what he warned would be the grave results of overruling *Betts v. Brady*. The right to counsel would be extended to the most trivial cases, he predicted, and the cost of providing all those lawyers for the poor would be "a tremendous burden on the taxpayers." The next thing you knew, poor people would also demand other free services to help prepare their defenses—doctors, investigators and experts. In effect, Jacob said, "this Court would be requiring the states to adopt socialism, or a welfare program."

He mentioned the survey he had made of Florida prisons, finding 5,093 prisoners who had not had lawyers. All of them, he warned, might get out if *Betts v. Brady* were overruled. He implored the Court not to let a victory for Gideon, if he won, be applied to those others in jail.

Chief Justice Warren asked whether some of those 5,093 Florida prisoners were illiterate—could not read or write. His point was clear—and dangerous to Jacob. Even under the rule of *Betts v. Brady* a man was supposed to be given a lawyer if he was illiterate. That was one of the "special circumstances."

"I have no way of knowing," Jacob replied.

"No, but what do you think?" the Chief Justice pressed. "Do you think most of them are literate or illiterate?" (The Court then had before it the petition Gideon had written for his illiterate fellow-prisoner, Allen Baxley Jr.)

"I don't know," Jacob said, "but I am sure some of them are illiterate."

When Jacob had finished, George Mentz stood up to argue for Alabama as a friend of the Court. He was an older man, gray-haired, more experienced than Jacob and much more at ease. Questions seemed to give him less pain. He answered in a charming Southern voice, making graceful admissions.

"I admit," Mentz said, "that it would be desirable for the states to furnish counsel in all criminal cases. But we say the states should have the right to make that decision themselves."

JUSTICE HARLAN: "Supposing Betts against Brady is not overruled. How many years is it going to take Alabama to pass a law like New York and the other states?"

MENTZ: "I don't know, but there is a growing feeling in the trial courts that something should be done."

Mentz then made the argument that poor men without lawyers "probably get off easier." A poor man "may get his story across to the jury better" than many lawyers, Mentz said.

JUSTICE BLACK: "That's not very complimentary to our profession."

MENTZ (good-humoredly): "No, sir."

JUSTICE HARLAN: "Supposing you had a choice of keeping Betts against Brady and then having a series of cases come to this Court, every one of which was reversed by finding special circumstances so that everyone would know we were only paying lip service to *Betts,* or else of overruling it."

131

MENTZ: "We'd rather see them decided case by case."

HARLAN: "Even though you know how all of them will come out."

MENTZ: "Hope springs eternal." (Laughter in the courtroom.)

Then Fortas got up for his rebuttal. He had saved a ringing statement for his conclusion.

"I think Betts against Brady was wrong when it was decided," Fortas said. "I think time has made that clear. And I think time has now made it possible for the correct rule, the civilized rule, the rule of American constitutionalism, the rule of due process to be stated by this Court with limited disturbance to the states."

CHAPTER 10
The Justices Decide

A T their Friday conference the justices discuss and vote on all cases on which they have heard oral argument earlier in the week. Then, within the next few days, the Chief Justice sends a note around to one member of the Court asking him to write the opinion; or he may keep that opinion to do himself. If there was disagreement in the conference about the case, and the Chief Justice was on the losing side, then the senior justice in the majority decides who is to write the opinion of the Court. Those in the minority get together and agree on one of them to write a dissenting opinion. But after these assignments are made, any justice may write a separate opinion on his own if he wishes, either agreeing with the majority or dissenting.

When a justice finishes the draft of an opinion, he sends it down to a print shop that operates in the basement of the Supreme Court. There it is put into type, and a very few copies are printed on galley proofs. The proofs are carefully numbered to keep track of them, so that none can get out to the outside world. They are then circulated around the Court, and the writer of each opinion receives comments from the other justices.

At this stage, minds may change. The justice assigned to write an opinion may find, after looking into the case more carefully, that the position he took at the Friday conference does not work out when he tries to write it. The majority may then agree to a change of position, or the opinion may be assigned to a different judge. Sometimes, when a dissenting opinion is sent around, it persuades enough justices so that the original minority becomes a majority. More often, the justice writing the majority opinion takes note of what the dissenters are saying and inserts in his opinion answers to their arguments.

Opinions of the Court are usually written in a careful style because the author has to worry about pleasing all the other justices in his majority. The dissenter, on the other hand, is free to express his personal views strongly, so that dissents have a more individual flavor. Charles Evans Hughes, who was Chief Justice from 1930 to 1941 and one of the great figures in the Court's history, said dissenting opinions were "an appeal to the brooding spirit of the law, to the intelligence of a future day, when a later decision may possibly correct the error" seen by the dissenting judge. His description fit the dissent written by Justice Black in 1942 in *Betts v. Brady*.

The whole process of discussion among the justices, voting and writing of opinions is entirely hidden from public view. It may go on for months. But no one except the justices and their law clerks—and some printers sworn to secrecy—have any knowledge of how a case is going to be decided until, one day, the opinions are announced in the courtroom. There are almost no news leaks at the Supreme Court—one of the many ways in which it differs from the other branches of government.

For the people involved in a case, and their lawyers, the period between argument and decision can be a time of tension, of might-have-beens, of daydreams and nightmares. Two months after the Gideon argument, at the beginning of March, 1963, Bruce Jacob was still thinking about the strangeness of that day.

"It was so different from the Florida Supreme

Court," he told a visitor. "They weren't concerned with precedents. Instead they had all those probing questions, trying to carry everything to its farthest point. I wanted to be honest. When they asked me whether there were some prisoners in Raiford [state prison] who should have had counsel, I had to say yes, because I had read some records and there were. But the more honest I was, the more they kept putting me on the spot. Some of the questions were just designed to embarrass our position. I never had judges make your side look as bad as it could.

"I had been working on this thing for months, but some of the questions were completely surprising. You could tell they knew what they were doing, that they were awfully smart men, that they had the benefit of the best thinking of the country."

Jacob had no doubt, now, that the Court would overrule *Betts v. Brady* and hold that Gideon should have had a lawyer. He wondered who was writing the opinion of the Court. It might have been assigned to a newer man, such as Justice Stewart, but Jacob thought not. He was sure Chief Justice Warren must have given Justice Black the pleasure of turning his 20-year-old dissent in *Betts v. Brady* into law.

It was only a few days later, as it happened, that the Gideon case was decided by the Supreme Court. There was no advance announcement. There never is. The Court does not hand out press releases before it does something, as other government agencies do. The justices just begin reading their opinions, and those interested have to be in the courtroom to hear what cases are being decided that day. Reading opinions aloud is a practice that most American courts have abandoned; to save time they just hand out printed copies. But there is special drama in hearing the justices of the Supreme Court personally announce their decisions. The justices, who disagree about so many things, have different ways of doing this, too. Some read the exact words of what they have written. Others give brief, condensed versions. Others, especially in important cases, go beyond the written words and explain the decision to the people in the courtroom.

The most junior justice who has a majority opinion always begins the reading, and the others follow, on up to the justice with the longest service and the Chief Justice. On Monday, March 18, 1963, the newest member of the Court, Justice Goldberg, had an opinion and so started off the reading. After him there were opinions by Justices Stewart, Brennan and Douglas.

As the justices read an opinion, page boys bring copies of the printed version around to a few persons at the front of the courtroom—the Solicitor General, who is the federal government's chief lawyer in the Supreme Court, and a handful of newspaper reporters. As they looked over the opinions being announced briefly by Justice Douglas that morning, they knew that they were about to learn the outcome of the Gideon case. For Justice Douglas referred in another case to *"Gideon v. Wainwright,* decided today." The formal title of the case had been changed from *Gideon v. Cochran* because the head of the Florida prison system, Cochran, had retired and been replaced by Louie L. Wainwright.

When Justice Douglas finished, it was Justice Black's turn to read any opinions he had ready. He looked at his wife, who was sitting in the box reserved for the justices' families and friends, and said: "I have for announcement the opinion and judgment of the Court in Number 155, Gideon against Wainwright."

Justice Black leaned forward and gave his words the emphasis and the emotion of a great occasion. Speaking very directly to the audience in the courtroom, in an almost folksy way, he told about Clarence Earl Gideon's case and how it had reached the Supreme Court of the United States.

"It raised a fundamental question," Justice Black said, "the rightness of a case we decided twenty-one years ago, Betts against Brady. When we granted certiorari in this case, we asked the lawyers on both sides to argue to us whether we should reconsider that case. We do reconsider Betts and Brady, and we reach an opposite conclusion."

Now Justice Black began reading sections of his written opinion. Quoting from the record of Gideon's trial, he said Gideon had handled "his defense about as well as could be expected" of someone who was not a lawyer. That was very much the same as had been said of Betts, and in fact the Gideon case was strikingly similar to *Betts v. Brady*. "Since the facts and circumstances of the two cases are so nearly indistinguishable," Justice Black said, "we think *Betts v. Brady,* if left standing, would require us to reject Gideon's claim that the Constitution guarantees him the assistance of counsel."

The rest of Justice Black's ten-page opinion was a smashing attack on *Betts v. Brady.* He did not try to show that the case had to be overruled because of something that had changed in the country or in the law since 1942. The earlier decision had just been wrong to start with. The right to a lawyer guaranteed in federal criminal trials by the Sixth Amendment was so "fundamental" that it was guaranteed in state cases by the Fourteenth Amendment.

"In our system of criminal justice," Justice Black said, "any person haled into court who is too poor to hire a lawyer cannot be assured a fair trial unless counsel is provided for him. This seems to us to be an obvious truth. Governments, both state and federal, quite properly spend vast sums of money to establish machinery to try defendants accused of crime.

Lawyers to prosecute are everywhere deemed essential to protect the public's interest in an orderly society. Similarly, there are few defendants charged with crime, few indeed, who fail to hire the best lawyers they can get to prepare and present their defenses. That government hires lawyers to prosecute and defendants who have money hire lawyers to defend are the strongest indications of the widespread belief that lawyers in criminal courts are necessities, not luxuries.

"The right of one charged with crime to counsel may not be deemed fundamental and essential to fair trials in some countries, but it is in ours."

Justice Black noted the brief for the twenty-three states saying that *Betts v. Brady* was wrong when handed down and should now be overruled. "We agree," he said.

The opinion ended in this legal language: "The judgment is reversed and the cause is remanded to the Supreme Court of Florida for action not inconsistent with this opinion." That meant that the Supreme Court was setting aside the Florida court's decision approving Gideon's conviction without a lawyer. The Florida court now had to take some action agreeable to what Justice Black had written in his opinion—probably to give Gideon a new trial, this time with a lawyer.

Justice Black's was not the only opinion in the

Gideon case. Three other justices wrote their own views separately, and stated them that day in court. But all agreed on the end result—that *Betts v. Brady* must be overruled. On that the Court was unanimous.

Justice Douglas signed the Black opinion. But in a short separate opinion he said he wished the Court would change its mind and accept the old argument that the entire Bill of Rights was "incorporated" into the Fourteenth Amendment and applied to the states. Justice Black had not mentioned this favorite idea of his, since he was happy enough to win on the single question of a poor man's right to counsel.

Justice Clark followed a different line of reasoning, not agreeing to the Black opinion. In a separate statement he pointed to his own 1960 opinion rejecting the idea that the Constitution prohibited military trials for American civilians overseas only when they faced the death penalty. There could be no constitutional distinction between capital cases and others, Justice Clark said. He noted that under *Betts v. Brady* the Supreme Court had absolutely required a lawyer in capital cases. By his reasoning, the Court must do the same in other cases. The Fourteenth Amendment protected a man's "liberty" and "property" as well as his "life."

Justice Harlan also took a legal path of his own. "I agree that *Betts v. Brady* should be overruled," he said, "but consider it entitled to a more respectful burial." He could not agree that it had been wrong when it was decided in 1942. But since then the rule of *Betts v. Brady*, that a man had to show "special circumstances" to obtain a free lawyer, had had "a troubled journey," Justice Harlan said. The Court had found "special circumstances" in every right-to-counsel case it had heard since *Quicksall v. Michigan* in 1950. "In truth the *Betts v. Brady* rule is no longer a reality," he said, but state courts had not "fully recognized" this and were still denying lawyers to the poor.

Then Justice Harlan harked back to the last question he had asked George Mentz at the argument of the Gideon case—whether it would not be better for the Supreme Court to adopt a new rule openly than to pay "lip service" to an old one that it really no longer believed. His opinion concluded: "To continue a rule which is honored by this Court only with lip service is not a healthy thing and in the long run will do disservice to the federal system."

That was the end of Clarence Earl Gideon's case in the Supreme Court of the United States. The opinions were quickly circulated around the country by special legal services, then issued in pamphlets by the Government Printing Office. Eventually they appeared in the bound volumes of Supreme Court decisions, which are called the United States Reports.

There the case is identified by lawyers as *Gideon v. Wainwright*, 372 U.S. 335—meaning that the opinions can be found beginning on page 335 of the 372nd volume of the reports.

Justice Black, talking to a friend a few weeks after the decision, said quietly: "When Betts against Brady was decided, I never thought I'd live to see it overruled."

CHAPTER 11

The Results
of Gideon's Case

THE day the Gideon case was decided, a friend in
Washington telephoned Bruce Jacob in Florida
to give him the news. "It's only the beginning,"
Jacob said. And he was right.

The Supreme Court had said that a poor man must
be given a lawyer for his defense in a serious criminal
trial. But the Court had not solved, and could not
solve, the practical problems that remained. Where
were all the necessary lawyers to come from? How
could the poor defendant be certain of getting an

able lawyer, experienced in criminal trials? Who would provide the needed money? Those questions had to be answered by the country's lawyers and judges and elected representatives. The Supreme Court had sounded a trumpet. The response had to come from the country.

Just how long it may take to live up to the promise of a Supreme Court decision can be shown by example. Twenty-five years before the Gideon case, the Court had made clear that poor defendants in *federal* criminal trials were always entitled to free counsel. But what was done to see to it that a fair, efficient system of providing those lawyers was set up in the federal courts? Practically nothing. Congress refused year after year to grant any money to pay lawyers for poor federal criminal defendants. No one kept a list of trained criminal lawyers who could be appointed in needy cases. When a federal judge found that a poor man was about to go to trial, all he could do was ask some lawyer whom he knew or had heard about or saw in the back of the courtroom to step in and represent the man. The choice was largely a matter of accident.

The result was that many poor men were represented by inadequate counsel. And the burden of serving poor defendants fell unfairly on a few lawyers. Senator Sam Ervin of North Carolina, writing in the American Bar Association Journal shortly after the Gideon decision, told what had happened to a lawyer out in Wyoming. A federal judge picked him to represent the defendant in a major criminal case. He had to spend ten days and three nights in court, and much other time getting ready. The prosecutor called 114 witnesses. The lawyer was in practice all alone, so he practically had to close down his office for six weeks to handle this case that was not going to pay him a penny. Senator Ervin said the lawyer almost went bankrupt.

Robert F. Kennedy, who was then Attorney General, told a committee of Congress in May, 1963, how badly the defense of the poor was arranged in federal courts. The job was given, he said, to lawyers who were not paid for their services or even given anything to cover their own expenses. They had no help from investigators or experts, who might for example be able to trace a gun that figured in a crime. They were likely to be appointed to defend a man long after his arrest, when witnesses had disappeared. And judges often picked "young, inexperienced lawyers, knowing little about the criminal law." Kennedy said it was sheer luck if this way of doing things worked fairly for either defendants or lawyers.

After twenty-five years, then, the federal courts still had a long way to go before they could claim to have an effective system of justice for the poor. And in the states the problem was much larger and more difficult.

The federal government brings only a handful of criminal prosecutions compared to the states—a few thousand a year as against perhaps a million state cases. The reason is that the Constitution leaves it mostly to the states to insure peace and order. Unless they take place in a federal area such as the District of Columbia, crimes like assault or robbery or murder are ordinarily matters for the states to punish. Moreover, there are relatively few federal courts, while the states have dozens of different kinds—traffic courts and justice-of-the-peace courts and special night courts and others. Because they deal with the dirty little crimes of our city life today—thievery and drunkenness and the like—state courts get a much larger percentage of down-and-out defendants with no money to hire a lawyer. In federal criminal cases about 33 per cent of the defendants cannot afford a lawyer. In state cases about 60 per cent of the defendants have no money for counsel.

The larger number of cases, the different kinds of courts and the greater percentage of poor defendants —all these made the job of assuring good lawyers for the poor a much harder one in state courts. And that was the job that the Supreme Court, in the Gideon case, said had to be done.

There were various ideas on how to go about it. Leading lawyers had been considering for years what the best system would be to assure counsel for the poor, and they were not agreed.

Some thought the solution was for each state or big city to hire a "public defender." That idea had first been tried in 1913, in Los Angeles, and by 1963 was in use in all or parts of thirteen states. The public defender is an official paid out of the people's taxes, just like the prosecutor. While the prosecutor and his staff work to see that the guilty are convicted, the public defender and his assistants defend suspected persons who cannot pay for their own lawyers. The great advantage of this system is that public defenders get plenty of practice in handling criminal cases. Poor defendants are sure of an experienced lawyer to stand up against an experienced prosecutor.

Others were uneasy about the public-defender plan. They did not like to have the lawyers on both sides of the same case employed by the government. They thought a private lawyer, owing nothing to any government, could fight for his client more vigorously. The cities and states that used public defenders rejected these criticisms. But most lawyers probably believed that the system of private counsel had worked well in our history and should be used for the problem of poor defendants if possible.

The trouble was that so few lawyers in private practice knew anything about criminal cases. Most of them worked on civil cases—contracts and wills and business problems—and considered the lawyers who went down to the criminal courtrooms just a little grubby. For these reasons, although the experts disagreed on how the states should arrange to provide lawyers under the new rule of the Gideon case, they did agree on some things. One was that the typical American lawyer should know more and do more about criminal law. As a student he should be encouraged to take an interest in criminal trials, and right after law school he should spend at least part of his time helping out in criminal courts and getting experience.

There was also widespread agreement that the busiest courts in our big cities had to have some group of lawyers regularly devoting their time to defense of the poor and being paid to do it. There were just too many cases to be handled by private lawyers in their spare time. If not public defenders, this office could be a private legal aid organization. In New York City, for example, the Legal Aid Society provided lawyers in 60,000 criminal cases a year. Its funds came from private contributions and also from the city treasury.

Where private lawyers were used, it was agreed by most experts, there should be some fair system of appointment. All the capable lawyers in a town might be put on a list and called in turn, for example, so that a few did not bear the whole burden. There was also agreement that when a man in private practice was appointed to represent a poor defendant, the state should at least pay him a little something and give him money for investigators and other expenses. Whether through public defenders or private counsel, then, the states should spend some money to assure a fair defense for poor men charged with crime. When the Gideon case was decided, many states spent nothing.

Thus it necessarily would take the efforts of legislatures and courts and lawyers and citizens to turn the ideal of *Gideon v. Wainwright* into reality. And those efforts did get under way after the Gideon case was decided, with surprising speed.

Members of the Supreme Court took every opportunity to preach the gospel of Gideon. At a lunch in May, 1963, Chief Justice Warren said representation of poor defendants was "a public responsibility." Whatever expense the states were put to, he said, would be worth while. Unfortunate citizens would get fairer treatment, and the states themselves would have criminal courts that worked more efficiently with the help of lawyers.

Several legal organizations launched the biggest projects in American history to try to solve the problem of legal services for poor defendants. They were given a total of $2,540,000 by the Ford Foundation to investigate what was being done all over the country, to improve law schools' teaching of criminal law and to set up model public-defender offices in a number of cities and towns.

In Washington, Congress finally acted to improve the situation in federal courts. At the urging of President Kennedy, money was provided for the first time to pay lawyers appointed for poor federal defendants and to pay the cost of investigators and other expenses. In the Criminal Justice Act of 1964, Congress directed every federal court to set up a system of counsel for the poor, either by keeping a list of private lawyers or by using a local legal-aid organization.

The states also reacted favorably and quickly to the Gideon decision. The most dramatic response came from Florida, which had so long refused to do anything for men like Clarence Earl Gideon. Shortly after the decision, Florida's governor, Farris Bryant, asked the state legislature to pass a public defender law. His words must have amused Gideon —because they came so late. In our day, the governor said, "it is unthinkable that an innocent man may be condemned to prison because he is unfamiliar with the intricacies of criminal procedure and unable to provide counsel for his defense." In May, 1963, barely two months after the Supreme Court had spoken, the Florida legislature passed a law calling for a public defender in each area of the state.

Other states voted money for private lawyers appointed to represent poor defendants. They extended the right of counsel to less serious cases. They took steps to see that poor men were not misled into saying they did not want a lawyer and so giving up their right. By three years after the Gideon decision, twenty-six states had made improvements in their methods of providing lawyers for the poor.

"Without the Supreme Court," Gideon had told his visitor in prison, "it might have happened sometime. But it wouldn't have happened in this state soon." The reaction to his case showed that he was right. For lawyers and members of state legislatures were taking steps that they now saw were essential to justice—but that they had not seen until the Supreme Court pointed them out. The Court, for its part, made clear that it would apply continuing pressure on the issue of the right to counsel. In the three months after the Gideon decision, during the rest of that Court term, it set aside thirty-one decisions of state courts and sent them back for a fresh look at prisoners' demands for counsel. One of these was the case of Allen Baxley Jr., the illiterate Florida prisoner whose petition Gideon had written.

When the Court reopened in the fall of 1963, after the summer recess, it dealt with one of the difficult problems that Justice Black had not mentioned in his opinion in the Gideon case—whether to apply the new rule to men already in prison. Ten Florida prisoners convicted without counsel before the Gideon decision asked for new trials now. The Court sent their cases back to Florida to be considered "in light of *Gideon v. Wainwright*." That was a hint, if not a direct order, that anyone deprived of counsel in the past must now have another chance. Florida took the hint. Anyone in the state's prisons who could show he had been denied a lawyer at his trial was taken out of jail and either tried again with a lawyer or, when officials thought it was no use retrying him, just let go. The results were spectacular. By a year after the Gideon decision, more than a thousand Florida prisoners had won their freedom. (Contrary to the fears of many officials, a crime wave did not result. Three years after the decision, fewer of the released prisoners had returned to crime than was usual for ex-convicts.)

It was a great task for America to bring to life the dream of *Gideon v. Wainwright*—the dream of a large and varied country in which every man charged with crime would be capably defended, no matter how poor he might be—and in which the lawyer representing him would do so proudly, sure of proper support and without resentment at an unfair burden. There would be a long road to travel before every criminal court in the United States lived up to the words that appear on the front of the Supreme Court building: *Equal Justice Under Law*. But the journey had begun.

CHAPTER 12

The Supreme Court and the People

THE case of *Gideon v. Wainwright* is partly a tribute to one human being. Against all the odds, Clarence Earl Gideon insisted that he should have a lawyer and kept on insisting all the way to the Supreme Court of the United States. His triumph there shows that the poorest and weakest of men —a convict with not even a friend to visit him in prison—can take his cause to the highest court in the land and bring about a great change in the law.

But of course Gideon was not alone. There were

working for him forces larger than he could understand in our law and our way of life. His case was part of a movement of history, and it will be read in that light by thousands of lawyers and judges who will know nothing about Clarence Earl Gideon except that he stood up in a Florida courtroom and said: "The United States Supreme Court says I am entitled to be represented by counsel."

That is the wonder of the law—that it moves case by case, seeking justice for each individual, but that any single case may be part of some larger movement. These great currents may not be noticed when they first start flowing, even by those who set them loose. It is doubtful that the justices of the Supreme Court had any idea that they were starting a constitutional revolution when they first ruled, in the case of the Scottsboro boys in 1932, that a criminal conviction in a state court violated the Constitution because it had been unfair not to provide lawyers for the defendants.

And it has been a revolution. In the three decades since the Scottsboro case, the law governing what state and local policemen and prosecutors may do in criminal cases has been wholly changed. At the beginning a state officer could say confidently that there were almost no limits in the federal Constitution on how he went about his job, and almost no chance that any conviction he won would be set aside by a federal court. Today a web of constitutional limitations covers the whole system of criminal law in the states, from arrest through trial and sentence to appeal. A state officer knows that a conviction may well be set aside if he has arrested the suspect illegally, forced a confession out of him, used evidence obtained illegally without a warrant, refused him a lawyer, put him through a prejudiced trial or denied him the right to appeal. All of these limits have been developed by the Supreme Court, case by case, by applying to new facts the vague promise of the Fourteenth Amendment—"due process of law."

Just as the Gideon case was part of a movement in the law of the right to counsel, and that in turn was part of all the changes taking place in the rules of fair criminal procedure, so this movement in the criminal law was part of a larger trend. In many other ways, over recent years, the Supreme Court has increased the liberty of the individual American citizen and his right to be free of state controls. The citizen can write and speak freely today, for example, knowing that the Supreme Court will protect him if anyone tries to jail him for what he says, unless he stirs violence. Even more significant have been the long series of decisions by the Court making clear that no state and no official may treat someone unfairly because of the color of his skin.

157

The Court has been severely criticized for many of its decisions upholding the dignity and freedom of the individual. The criticism is often unfair and nasty to the justices, but it would be a mistake to think that the Supreme Court should be above criticism. The Court has great power over American life, just as Congress and the President do, and like them it must face criticism. Unlike political leaders, the justices of the Supreme Court cannot answer the critics themselves; they must stay in their quiet building, not taking part in public debate. But others who care about the law must always consider whether it is right for the Court to be doing what it does.

Why should nine lawyers, appointed and not elected, play so big a part in a country that calls itself a democracy, ruled by the people? Is it proper that the Supreme Court, rather than elected representatives, should remake the country's procedure in criminal cases? Those are the questions raised by the Gideon case—or any other case involving the Supreme Court's extraordinary power to measure the actions of the states and the federal government against the Constitution and find them unlawful.

The answer given by our history is that, with all the power that governments have over people's lives, we need the balancing power of the Supreme Court to step in on behalf of individual freedom. There are many separate reasons for saying this.

The Supreme Court is often the only part of government that will listen to the unfortunate Americans, the poor and the despised. One example is Clarence Earl Gideon. No one else in government would really have cared about the fairness of his trial, not the Florida legislature and not Congress in Washington. Criminals and suspected criminals should not have any influence with our elected representatives. But it is good for all of us to see that even the worst sinners are treated fairly. The Supreme Court is our conscience on that.

In its decisions the Court also serves the purpose of awakening the conscience of other branches of government and of American citizens generally to national problems. Certainly the concern about the right to counsel shown by President Kennedy and Congress and the Ford Foundation and many lawyers' associations in 1963 grew out of the Court's decisions over the years.

When the machinery of our democratic system breaks down and there is no way for the voters to make repairs, the Court can help effectively. A notable example was the *Reapportionment Cases* of the 1960's. In both Congress and the state legislatures there were too many representatives from farm areas and not enough from cities and their suburbs. As America's population had moved more and more from the country into the big cities, the city people had not been given their full share of representatives. The men who were in office simply refused to change this. Finally, in the *Reapportionment Cases,* the Supreme Court stepped in and said it was a violation of the Constitution to have one representative for a hundred people in the country and another for a thousand people in the city. The States had to reapportion—give everyone an equal share in electing representatives.

But it is not enough of a defense of the Supreme Court to say that it corrects the failures of the other branches of government. That might possibly be done by someone else. The advantage of the Supreme Court is the *process* it applies to our national problems—the distinctive way it goes about its work.

One special feature of the Supreme Court, shown in the Gideon case, is the fact that it focuses on individual human beings. Congress does not and cannot do that. It debates large bills that have to be written in general terms, not referring to any particular citizen. By contrast, the Court under the Constitution can only consider cases involving the real interest of particular individuals. In an age that seems to be growing less human all the time, with huge impersonal corporations and government bureaus and bombs that can wipe out millions, surely it is good to have a Court that worries about the individual.

The smallness and personal character of the Court distinguish it from other government agencies, too. In the typical government department an idea has to work its way up through channels and committees, and the end result is likely to be a decision of the department, not of any individual. Supreme Court justices do their own work, as Brandeis said, and they take personal responsibility for every decision. Anyone who has ever tried to correct a mistake made by a government department knows how he has to fight his way through office after office, each one denying that it is responsible. In the Supreme Court the lawyer for a Gideon can speak directly to the justices and tell them why he thinks they should change something they have decided in the past.

An important quality of the Supreme Court is that it has to give reasons for what it decides. A mayor or Congressman or President does many things without explaining exactly why. He has to, because he must make political compromises between opposing pressure groups. But a court can never say: "X wins the case because he put more pressure on us." It has to give reasons that appeal to people's sense of fairness and justice. There are no secret ways to influence Supreme Court justices. Arguments are

161

made in open court, and the justices' opinions are public.

The Supreme Court is able to operate free of the political pressures of the moment because of a wise provision in the constitution. A justice, once appointed, holds his seat "during good behavior"—which in practical terms means until he decides to resign or retire. He does not have to run for election, and so he does not have to try to be popular. He is free to decide as his intelligence and his conscience demand. That helps to explain why men so often seem to change when they put on the black robes of a Supreme Court justice. Perhaps a Senator personally does not believe in denying civil rights to Negroes but feels that he has to make speeches against civil rights because that is what the majority of voters in his state want to hear. But if the President appoints him to the Supreme Court, he does not have to worry about being re-elected and can say what he really believes.

The independence given to the justices allows them to do things that other people know are right but have not had the courage or determination to do by themselves. Shortly before the Gideon case was decided, Abe Fortas was having lunch with a Pennsylvania lawyer in the cafeteria in the Supreme Court building. Pennsylvania was then the largest state that did not provide free lawyers for poor defendants in serious criminal cases. Fortas's luncheon companion said to him: "I've told the lawyers of my state and the officials again and again that they should make the appointment of counsel compulsory. They all know it in their hearts. But they won't move until this great institution tells them to."

Just as their right to sit on the Court for life protects the justices from political pressures, so are they cut loose from local prejudices. It is a natural tendency for a member of a state legislature or a state judge to put his state first in his mind and not think about the interest of the United States as a whole. Even members of Congress spend a lot of their time trying to do favors for their own states. But when a man becomes a Supreme Court justice, he has to make decisions for all the country, not any one part of it, and his mind inevitably begins to see things in a national way.

Of our high officers of government, only the President and the justices of the Supreme Court speak for the whole country and are free of ties to any section. It is essential that they should be. The United States today is more than ever a single nation, not a collection of states each going its own way. It has heavy responsibilities to protect peace and freedom all over the world. Its big companies span the country and cannot do their work inside just one state. Telephones and radio and television connect us all and make us consider ourselves Americans first, Californians or Kentuckians second. None of this would have been possible without the existence of a national Supreme Court to overcome divisions and prejudices among the states. Justice Holmes was not exaggerating when he said he did not think the United States could have survived as a Union without the unifying influence of the Supreme Court.

The Supreme Court decides problems more important and more difficult than any other court in the history of the world. A justice brings to the job only his honor, his intelligence, his education, his experience, his human understanding, his imagination. There really are no mysteries about the job. No one teaches a course on how to be a Supreme Court justice. It is not a place for specialists. Indeed, the Court stands for the idea that final decisions should not be left to experts, because they may know only their own field and not understand what the general public needs. We deliberately arrange, in the Supreme Court, for specialized problems to be given a dose of common sense.

That is one of the most curious things about the Supreme Court. Though the justices seem isolated in their cold marble building, they must be in touch with the basic feelings of the American people.

Justice Frankfurter wrote once that it was the

Supreme Court's duty to discover "the conscience of society." By that he did not mean that the Court should take a public-opinion poll and find out what popular feeling was about each issue from moment to moment. The Court must not be swayed by temporary popular emotions. Rather, Justice Frankfurter meant, the justices must sense the deeper ideal of the country. Those ideals slowly change in history. For example, many Americans used to be unconcerned when people were segregated on account of their race. But after Adolf Hitler had murdered millions of men, women and children simply because they were Jewish, more Americans began to think how dangerous it was to mistreat people in any way because of their race. Again, the rights of defendants in criminal cases did not seem so important years ago. But when Americans had seen the way dictators in other countries sent innocent men off to jail without fair trials, they cared more about protecting the rights of anyone charged with a crime.

The Supreme Court must reflect change and growth in the understanding of the American people. The Court is able to do that in part because, from time to time, new justices take the place of those who retire—younger men, trained differently as lawyers, brought up in a changed way of life, and therefore reflecting the spirit of a newer day. The men on the Court should also keep their minds open to new ideas, hard as that always is, and be willing to change their views.

The Court does not just reflect American ideals. It also leads opinion, educating the people and awakening their consciences. At its best the Court is a great teacher. It throws new light on questions such as the right of a poor man to a lawyer, and citizens who have not worried about that issue before take an interest. As the country comes to understand why it is unfair to make men defend themselves, or unfair to mistreat men because of their race, the Court may build on that understanding and take another step.

What is given to the justices is the opportunity not to command but to persuade. When the Court is unable to persuade the country in the long run that a decision is wise, the decision cannot really become a permanent part of our law. It will eventually be overruled or allowed to wither away. When the Supreme Court has lost touch with the true spirit of America, it has only damaged itself. Back in 1857, justices who thought they knew best said in the *Dred Scott Case* that Congress could not forbid slavery in the pioneer country in the West. In the Civil War the people decided that the Court was wrong. That is the risk the Court takes—the risk of failure.

When *Betts v. Brady* was decided in 1942, the six justices in the majority thought they had established a good rule. But trial and error—the case-by-case method of the law—showed that the rule did not work. When the Court in the Gideon case overthrew the *Betts* approach of "special circumstances" and said that every poor man facing a serious criminal charge must have a lawyer, it was giving the judgment of history.

Gideon v. Wainwright was a victory for Justice Black. But in a way the case shows that there was not necessarily so deep a division between him and Justice Frankfurter as may have appeared. Justice Frankfurter did believe much more deeply in the independence of the states, but he also thought that the Supreme Court must not let the states stray too far from national ideals of fairness—and he knew that those ideals gradually changed. Once he said: "It is of the very nature of a free society to advance in its standards of what is deemed reasonable and right." Perhaps *Betts v. Brady* was a matter of timing for him. He might have said in 1942 that the country was not prepared for a rule requiring lawyers for the poor in every serious criminal case, that state officials and lawyers and the people generally did not accept that ideal. But what would he have said if he had still been on the Court when it decided the Gideon case in 1963?

A few days after the decision, Justice Black visited Justice Frankfurter at home in his sick bed. He told

167

Justice Frankfurter about a conversation with the other members of the Court before they decided the Gideon case. He had told them, Justice Black said, that if Felix Frankfurter had still been there he would have voted to reverse the conviction of Clarence Earl Gideon and overrule *Betts v. Brady*.

Justice Frankfurter said: "Of course I would."

EPILOGUE:
Retrial

CLARENCE Earl Gideon had won his fight to give new meaning to the Constitution of the United States, but his own struggle was not over. He could have a new trial now, with a lawyer to defend him. Would he be found guilty of breaking into the Bay Harbor Poolroom? The answer to that question would not be a great constitutional decision, but it was important to Gideon. And, in a way, it was important to all the other Americans who believed along with him in the poor man's right to counsel.

For it might show whether a lawyer really made a difference.

The Supreme Court mailed the official notice of its decision to the Florida Supreme Court in April, 1963. On May 15 the Florida court ordered a new trial for Gideon. The trial was set for July 5, in the Panama City courtroom where Gideon had originally been convicted.

The next thing Gideon had to do was find a lawyer. That may have seemed easy, now that he had the right. But Gideon had shown that he could be a stubborn man, set in ways that seemed peculiar to other people, and he was about to show that again.

Abe Fortas, after winning the case in the Supreme Court, sent Gideon a last letter. He said he had asked a Florida lawyer for the American Civil Liberties Union, Tobias Simon, to help Gideon from then on. Simon was in Miami, the biggest and busiest and richest city in Florida—about as different as could be imagined from quiet Panama City, 600 miles away. When Gideon wrote to Simon, "humbly asking for help," Simon agreed to represent him.

On July 4, Independence Day, Simon went to Panama City with an experienced Miami criminal lawyer, Irwin J. Block, who had agreed to help him. They went to see Gideon, who had been brought to the local jail, and got the surprise of their lives. Gideon shouted at them, said he didn't want them and told them to go away.

"Gideon refused to be represented by either of us," Simon reported sadly to the American Civil Liberties Union. "All efforts to calm him and to have him place some trust in us failed."

The next morning—the morning set for the trial—they talked it over with the judge in his office. It was Judge Robert L. McCrary Jr., the same as at the first trial. Gideon was there, too. Judge McCrary began by noting that he had some papers signed by Simon as defense counsel.

"I didn't authorize Mr. Simon to sign anything for me," Gideon said. "I'll do my own signing. I do not want him to represent me."

Judge McCrary looked worried. "Do you want another lawyer to represent you?" he asked.

"No," said Gideon. "I want to plead my own case. I want to make my own plea. I do not want them to make any plea for me."

Here was the man who had insisted all the way to the Supreme Court that he had to have a lawyer—and now he was saying that he wanted to defend himself again. Judge McCrary was amazed, and no wonder. Just to make sure that he was not dreaming all this, he asked Gideon once more: "You don't want Mr. Simon and Mr. Block to represent you?"

"No," said Gideon. "I DO NOT WANT THEM." He spoke so firmly that the court stenographer, who

171

was there taking it all down, used capital letters.

Simon said he and Block had only wanted to help Gideon but of course would not stay against his wishes. Judge McCrary thanked them and let them go. But he also made clear that he was not going to let Clarence Earl Gideon be tried again in his courtroom without a lawyer.

The judge asked whether there was someone else Gideon would like to represent him. And it turned out there was—W. Fred Turner of Panama City, one of the town's most experienced lawyers in criminal trials.

Judge McCrary agreed quickly, before Gideon could change his mind again. "I am going to appoint Mr. Fred Turner," he said, "to represent this defendant." Then he put the trial off for a month so that Turner, who knew nothing about the case, would have time to get ready. The judge also offered to let Gideon go free during that month if he could put up $1,000 as bail money. But Gideon could not; so he went back to the state prison at Raiford until August 5, when he was brought down to Panama City again for the trial.

At 9:00 on the morning of August 5, 1963, in the Bay County Courthouse, Judge McCrary announced for the second time "the case of State of Florida versus Clarence Earl Gideon." He asked, just as he had two years before, "Is the state ready for trial?" The original prosecutor, Assistant State Attorney William E. Harris, was there and answered yes. This time the defendant was ready, too. Gideon sat at a table with Fred Turner, a thin, springy man forty-one years old. "We're ready, your Honor," Turner said, rolling a pencil briskly between his hands.

A jury of six men was chosen first. That took nearly an hour, because Turner—unlike Gideon when he was defending himself—questioned each juror to see if he was prejudiced. Turner kept two men off the jury because he thought they might be.

The prosecution had the same star witness, Henry Cook. He turned out to be a youth—twenty-two years old, with greasy black hair and sideburns down his cheeks. Under questioning by prosecutor Harris he told the same story as at the first trial. He had been at a dance in Apalachicola, been driven back to Bay Harbor by some friends in an "old model Chevrolet" at 5:30 in the morning and had seen Gideon inside the poolroom. Then, Cook said, Gideon had gone out, called a taxi and driven off.

But the cross-examination by Turner was quite different from the cross-examination by Gideon himself in the first trial.

Why, Turner asked, did the boys who had driven Cook back in that old Chevrolet leave him in front of the poolroom? Why hadn't they taken him to his home, which was just two blocks away?

173

"I was going to hang around the poolroom," Cook mumbled in a low voice, "till it opened up—seven o'clock."

Under further questioning Cook said he had been drinking beer in Apalachicola, until the stores closed at midnight. This brought Turner back to the question of what Cook had been doing at the Bay Harbor Poolroom at 5:30 in the morning. Turner's question was an accusation.

"Mr. Cook," he asked, "did you go into the Bay Harbor Poolroom?"

"No, sir."

"Did you all get a six-pack of beer out of there?"

"No, sir."

Cook did not mention calling the police after supposedly seeing Gideon in the poolroom. He said he had just walked to the corner and back. It was only later, when the police asked him, that he had given them Gideon's name. Turner, sounding doubtful, asked whether all that was true. Cook said it was.

"Ever been convicted of a felony?" Turner asked suddenly.

"No, sir, not convicted," Cook said. "I stole a car and was put on probation."

With that, Turner let him leave the witness stand. Turner had done what he wanted—raised some doubts in the jury's mind about how reliable a witness Henry Cook was.

The prosecution had one other important witness. He was Duell Pitts, a police detective who had investigated the break-in at the Bay Harbor Poolroom on the morning of June 3, 1961. He had questioned Cook, he said, got Gideon's name and finally found Gideon in a downtown Panama City bar and arrested him. Gideon's pockets were full of coins—$25.28 in quarters, dimes, nickels and a few pennies. The prosecutor suggested that the coins must have come from the juke box and the cigarette machine that had been opened in the poolroom.

For the defense, Turner had one surprise witness, the owner of the grocery in Bay Harbor, J. D. Henderson. On the morning of July 3, 1961, Henderson said, Henry Cook had come into the store and said "the law had picked him up for questioning" about the poolroom break-in.

"Picked who up?" Turner asked, pretending to be surprised.

"Henry Cook."

In other words, according to Henderson, Henry Cook had once indicated that he himself was under suspicion.

The second and last witness for the defense was Clarence Earl Gideon, taking the stand for the first time in his case. These were some of Fred Turner's questions and Gideon's answers:

TURNER: "On the morning of June 3, 1961, did

175

you break into and enter the Bay Harbor Poolroom?"

GIDEON: "No, sir."

TURNER: "What was the purpose of your going into town [after calling the taxi that morning]?"

GIDEON: "To get me another drink."

TURNER: "Where'd you get the money?"

GIDEON: "I gambled."

TURNER: "What kind of games?"

GIDEON: "Mostly rummy."

TURNER: "Did you ever gamble with Henry Cook?"

GIDEON: "Sure, I gambled with all those boys."

TURNER: "Did you have any wine with you?"

GIDEON: "I don't drink wine."

TURNER: "Any beer? Any Coke?"

GIDEON: "No."

TURNER: "What do you say to this charge that you broke and entered the pool hall?"

GIDEON: "I'm not guilty of it—I know nothing about it."

Then it was the prosecutor's turn to cross-examine. Harris asked where Gideon had been employed at the time of the crime, where he was working. "I wasn't employed," Gideon said. "I was gambling." There followed some questions about gambling that Gideon answered with a puzzled look, as if he could not understand Harris's lack of knowledge on the subject.

HARRIS: "Why did you have all that money in coins?"

176

GIDEON: "I've had as much as one hundred dollars in my pockets in coins."

HARRIS: "Why?"

GIDEON: "Have you ever run a poker game?"

HARRIS: "You would carry one hundred dollars in coins around for a couple of days at a time?"

GIDEON: "Yes, sir, I sure wouldn't leave it in my room in the Bay Harbor Hotel."

HARRIS: "Did you play rummy that night?"

GIDEON: "No—I was too busy drinking."

HARRIS: "Have you ever been convicted or pled guilty to a felony?"

GIDEON: "Yes, five times, including this one."

In the early afternoon the witnesses finished. Now Turner made his final speech to the jury. He was the model of the experienced criminal lawyer, dramatic but not too dramatic. His strategy was to throw suspicion on Henry Cook.

"This probationer," Turner said scornfully, referring to Cook's admission that he had stolen a car, "has been out at a dance drinking beer. . . . He does a peculiar thing [when he supposedly sees Gideon inside the poolroom]. He doesn't call the police, he just walks to the corner and walks back. . . . What happened to the beer and the wine and the Cokes? I'll tell you—it left the poolroom in that old model Chevrolet. The beer ran out at midnight in Apalachicola. . . . Why was Cook walking back and forth?

I'll give you the explanation: he was the lookout."

Turner had as good as accused Cook and his friends of the crime. Now he turned to Gideon.

"Gideon's a gambler," he said, "and he'd been drinking whiskey. I submit to you that he did just what he said that morning—he walked out of his hotel and went to that telephone booth to call a cab. . . . Cook saw him, and here was a perfect answer for Cook. He names Gideon."

Prosecutor Harris scoffed at Turner's speech. "There's no evidence here," he told the jury, "that Cook and his friends took this beer and wine." He brought the jury's mind back to the coins in Gideon's pocket when he was arrested. "Twenty-five dollars' worth of change," Harris said. "That's a lot to carry in your pocket. But Mr. Gideon carried one hundred dollars' worth of change in his pocket." He paused and raised his eyebrows. "Do you believe that?"

At 4:20 P.M. the jury went out to make up its mind. The prosecutors were confident. Harris's chief, State Attorney J. Frank Adams, was there watching because the case had become so famous. He still thought it was an easy case. "If Gideon had had a lawyer in the first place," Adams said, "he'd have been advised to plead guilty." But when half an hour passed and the jury was still out, the prosecutors began looking a little less confident.

The jurors filed back into the courtroom at 5:25.

178

They had their verdict written on a slip of paper, and the court clerk read it out. It was *Not Guilty*.

"So say you all?" asked Judge McCrary. The members of the jury nodded.

Judge McCrary had written of Gideon's first trial: "In my opinion he did as well as most lawyers could have done in handling his case." But Gideon had not done as well as Fred Turner. He had none of Fred Turner's training, or his experience in the courtroom, or his knowledge of Panama City and its people. He could not prepare the case as Turner had, because he had been in jail. Turner had spent three full days before the second trial investigating and talking to people about the case. Actually, he already knew a good bit about the prosecution's star witness, Henry Cook, because he had been Cook's lawyer once and successfully defended him against a charge of beating up a drunken man and robbing him of $1.98. Gideon's stubborn insistence on having a local lawyer may well have made the difference. It was doubtful that lawyers from Miami could have been as persuasive with a Panama City jury as Fred Turner.

Gideon was a free man now. He stood in the courtroom, tears in his eyes, and accepted congratulations from a few well-wishers. He said he hoped to see his children the next day, then go off to stay with a friend in Tallahassee, Florida. That night he would pay a last, triumphant visit to the Bay Harbor Poolroom. Could someone let him have a few dollars? Someone did.

"Do you feel you accomplished something?" a newspaper reporter asked.

"Well I did."

Afterword: 1972

I T is now ten years since Clarence Earl Gideon's letter from prison arrived at the Supreme Court. His case is history, but it is living history. Time has not diminished the importance of the constitutional law made by the Supreme Court in Gideon's name. His case is still resounding in the courtrooms of America.

The most direct and immediate effect has naturally been to bring lawyers into many cases where poor men and women would previously have faced criminal charges without trained assistance. And that change has come about not just in Florida, where Gideon was, and other states that formerly provided lawyers only in cases involving the death sentence.

New York, for example, has felt the effect of the Gideon decision keenly. New York always did allow free counsel for the poor in all serious criminal trials, the felony cases; but in practice many defendants did not realize they were entitled to a lawyer. In a state as supposedly up-to-date as New York, many poor people still defended themselves against criminal charges. But in the last decade, all that has dramatically changed: The overwhelming majority of poor criminal defendants now do get lawyers. In New York City most of them come from the Legal Aid Society, which has a large permanent staff and operates with support from the city budget.

In fact, by 1968 four-fifths of *all* defendants in New York City were provided with free lawyers. That proved what the justices of the Supreme Court had believed—that most men and women charged with crime are poor people, the very ones who need a lawyer's advice the most. After Gideon's case many more of them did have a lawyer's help when they needed it. The gradual change over ten years has not by any means given the poor man as good a chance in the courtroom as the rich. Usually, in a place as overcrowded as the criminal courts of New York, the poor defendant can have only a hurried conversation with his lawyer before his case is called. That is still not justice. The whole process of the criminal law in too many crowded city systems is still a disgrace. But a start has been made on the Supreme Court's promise: "Equal justice under law."

And the Gideon decision led the Supreme Court on to related issues. One was whether a poor person should have a right to a free lawyer when charged with a misdemeanor—a less serious criminal offense. The charge against Gideon himself had been a felony, with the weighty sentence of five years in prison, but the Court in deciding the case had not said specifically that the Constitution guaranteed lawyers only in felony cases.

If a poor man was charged with disorderly conduct, facing a sentence of only a few days in jail at most, should the state have to give him a lawyer? Or suppose he was accused of dangerous driving? If lawyers had to be provided, the demand would certainly be much greater. That was what the Supreme Court had to weigh as it considered whether to extend the Gideon rule to petty offenses.

Another important question left unanswered in the Gideon decision was *when* the right to a lawyer began. Could the poor man call for free legal advice the minute he was arrested and the police began questioning him, or did he have to wait until he was in the courtroom? That question was answered in 1966 in another extremely important decision of the Supreme Court: *Miranda v. Arizona.* The Court decided that before a policeman began questioning a suspect, he must tell the arrested person that he or she had a right to see a lawyer first—and must supply a free one if the suspect was poor.

The Miranda case brought a flood of criticism on the Supreme Court. Americans on the whole seemed to agree with the general idea of a right to counsel for poor defendants, and the Gideon decision won wide praise. But it was a very different matter to bring lawyers into the police station. Some police were afraid that they could not get a suspect to answer questions if he had a lawyer's advice first, because a lawyer would almost certainly advise him to say nothing. That would mean fewer confessions, fewer convictions, more unsolved crimes. This concern on the part of the police had a great deal of support among the American people generally. For the 1960's were a time of sharply rising crime in the United States—of robberies and thefts and muggings, of rapidly increasing drug addiction and widespread fear of walking in the streets of the great cities.

It was not only the Miranda case that caused controversy. The whole trend of Supreme Court decisions in favor of greater rights for the accused person began to arouse a "backlash." The public, alarmed by the increase in crime, took to blaming the courts. The argument was that judges were being too easy on suspected criminals—too soft-hearted, too sentimental—and were thereby encouraging crime.

Investigation did not really bear out these attacks on judges. Experts who studied the problem said that the constitutional rights newly declared by the Supreme Court, such as the right to counsel, had little if any effect on the mind of the addict who decided to mug someone. The reason for the terrible American crime statistics lay elsewhere: in our crumbling city life, our racial tensions, our failure to deal with the drug problem, our overburdened police, our out-of-date court system and appalling prisons.

But public doubts about the Supreme Court's decisions on the rights of criminal defendants grew over the years. Political leaders, sensing the concern, became increasingly critical of the Court. In 1968 Richard Nixon, the Republican candidate for President, pledged in his campaign to restore "law and order" to the country—for one thing, by appointing Supreme Court justices who would take a tougher attitude toward suspected criminals.

The Court itself was closely divided. In the Gideon case it had been unanimous, but the vote in the Miranda case was 5 to 4. Soon after Richard Nixon was elected, the chance came to change that majority. And by a great irony, that chance involved one of the actors in the drama of the Gideon case: Abe Fortas.

When the Supreme Court appointed Abe Fortas to argue Clarence Gideon's case, he was one of the most successful and influential lawyers in Washington. Three years later President Johnson picked him to become a Supreme Court justice himself. He replaced Arthur Goldberg, who left the Court at the President's request to become Ambassador to the United Nations. President Johnson made the announcement on July 28, 1965, describing Fortas as "one of the nation's most able and most respected and most outstanding citizens, a scholar, a profound thinker, a lawyer of superior ability and a man of humane and deeply compassionate feelings." The Senate approved the nomination with just three dissenting votes.

As a justice, Abe Fortas proved to be a liberal and a powerful thinker. One of his great contributions came in the 1967 case of Gerald Gault, a fifteen-year-old boy who went before a juvenile court without a lawyer and was ordered to be committed for up to six years. Justice Fortas's opinion for a majority of the Court said that a young person facing serious charges had the same constitutional rights as others—the right to a lawyer, the right to know the charges against him, the right to confront his accusers and cross-examine them. It was an opinion that amounted to a partial Bill of Rights for young people.

On June 26, 1968, President Johnson announced that Earl Warren was retiring as Chief Justice of the United States and that Justice Abe Fortas would replace him. But the promotion to Chief Justice required the approval of the Senate, and in an election year the Republicans (who hoped to win the White House) were reluctant to approve such an important nomination. They used the occasion to attack Fortas and the Court. On October 2, 1968, Justice Fortas withdrew his name as nominee for Chief Justice so as to end, he said, "destructive and extreme assaults upon the Court." He remained an Associate Justice.

The following May it was publicly disclosed that in 1965, after going on the Court, Justice Fortas had made a private financial arrangement with the family foundation of a businessman named Louis Wolfson. For "continuing services," the foundation was to pay $20,000 annually to Justice Fortas or, if he died, to his wife. One payment was made before Justice Fortas decided to return it and cancel the agreement.

In the meantime Mr. Wolfson had been convicted of federal criminal charges connected with the stock market, and he had consulted Justice Fortas several times. On May 15, 1969, Justice Fortas resigned from the Supreme Court. He wrote Chief Justice Warren that he did so "in order that the Court may not continue to be subjected to extraneous stress which may adversely affect the performance of its important functions."

That vacancy on the Supreme Court set off a long political struggle between President Nixon and the Senate. Twice the President nominated Southern judges—Clement Haynsworth of South Carolina and G. Harrold Carswell of Florida—and twice the Senate rejected them as unfit for the Court. Then the President named, and the Senate at last confirmed, Judge Harry Blackmun of Minnesota. At the same time, Chief Justice Warren's retirement became effective, and in his place came Warren E. Burger of Minnesota, who had been serving as a judge of the U.S. Court of Appeals in Washington, D.C.

Chief Justice Burger and Justice Blackmun both turned out to be more conservative judges than the men they replaced, and especially conservative about the criminal law. They quickly made clear that they thought the old Court had gone too far in interpreting the Constitution to protect those accused of crime.

In 1971 two of the most distinguished members of the Court died: Hugo Black and John Marshall Harlan. To fill those vacancies President Nixon appointed, and the Senate confirmed, two more conservatives, Lewis Powell of Virginia and William Rehnquist of Arizona.

The balance had changed among those nine men who read and explain the American Constitution, applying its old words to new problems. The day of experiment in new rights for the criminal accused seemed to be over, for a time at least. But there would be no turning back on one most basic right: the right to a lawyer. The new members of the Supreme Court, like the old, made it clear that the case of *Gideon v. Wainwright* would remain a fixed star of the Constitution.

And what of Clarence Earl Gideon? After his great legal victory, new friends helped him to find work in Florida. But eventually he drifted away, returning to his life as a wanderer. He had one small brush with the law, in 1965, when he went to the Kentucky Derby, lost all his money betting on the horses and was arrested for vagrancy; he spent a night in jail. Then he faded out of the limelight, and the world did not hear of him again until 1972. On January 18 of that year, Clarence Gideon, aged sixty-one, died in a Fort Lauderdale, Florida, hospital. On the hospital admission form, he had given his mother's name and address. Hospital officials telephoned her in Hannibal, Missouri, and she sent for the body. Clarence Earl Gideon was buried in Hannibal.

His mother expressed regret that her son, many years earlier, had run away from home and school and become a wanderer. She said, "He could have been most anything if he'd gone to school as he ought to, and behaved himself."

But he *was* something. That is why, as long as the United States has a Constitution and a Supreme Court, Clarence Earl Gideon will be remembered.

THE BILL OF RIGHTS AND THE FOURTEENTH AMENDMENT

The first ten amendments to the United States Constitution are often called "The Bill of Rights." Proposed on September 25, 1789, they were declared in force on December 15, 1791.

The Fourteenth Amendment, proposed on June 13, 1866, was proclaimed on July 28, 1868. The first of its five sections is reprinted here.

AMENDMENT 1

Congress shall make no law respecting an establishment of religion, or prohibiting the free exercise thereof; or abridging the freedom of speech, or of the press; or the right of the people peaceably to assemble, and to petition the Government for a redress of grievances.

AMENDMENT 2

A well regulated Militia, being necessary to the security of a free State, the right of the people to keep and bear Arms, shall not be infringed.

AMENDMENT 3

No Soldier shall, in time of peace, be quartered in any house, without the consent of the Owner, nor in time of war, but in a manner to be prescribed by law.

AMENDMENT 4

The right of the people to be secure in their persons, houses, papers, and effects, against unreasonable searches and seizures, shall not be violated, and no Warrants shall issue, but upon probable cause, supported by Oath or affirmation, and particularly describing the place to be searched, and the persons or things to be seized.

AMENDMENT 5

No person shall be held to answer for a capital, or otherwise infamous crime, unless on a presentment or indictment of a Grand Jury, except in cases arising in the land or naval forces, or in the Militia, when in actual service in time of War or public danger; nor shall any person be subject for the same offence to be twice put in jeopardy of life or limb; nor shall be compelled in any Criminal Case to be a witness against himself, nor be deprived of life, liberty, or property, without due process of law; nor shall private property be taken for public use, without just compensation.

AMENDMENT 6

In all criminal prosecutions, the accused shall enjoy the right to a speedy and public trial, by an impartial jury of the State and district wherein the crime shall have been committed, which district shall have been previously ascertained by law, and to be informed of the nature and cause of the accusation; to be confronted with the witnesses against him; to have compulsory process for obtaining Witnesses in his favor, and to have the Assistance of Counsel for his defence.

AMENDMENT 7

In suits at common law, where the value in controversy shall exceed twenty dollars, the right of trial by jury shall be preserved, and no fact tried by a jury shall be otherwise re-examined in any Court of the United States, than according to the rules of the common law.

AMENDMENT 8

Excessive bail shall not be required, nor excessive fines imposed, nor cruel and unusual punishments inflicted.

AMENDMENT 9

The enumeration in the Constitution, of certain rights, shall not be construed to deny or disparage others retained by the people.

AMENDMENT 10

The powers not delegated to the United States by the Constitution, nor prohibited by it to the States, are reserved to the States respectively, or to the people.

*   *   *   *

AMENDMENT 14, Section 1

All persons born or naturalized in the United States, and subject to the jurisdiction thereof, are citizens of the United States and of the State wherein they reside. No State shall make or enforce any law which shall abridge the privileges or immunities of citizens of the United States; nor shall any State deprive any person of life, liberty, or property, without due process of law; nor deny to any person within its jurisdiction the equal protection of the laws.

A GLOSSARY OF LEGAL TERMS

AMICUS CURIAE: Friend of the court (from the Latin): someone who is not personally involved in a case but who is interested and gives the court his views in a *brief* or an *oral argument* or both.

APPEAL: Request to a higher court, made by the side that lost in a lower court, to review the lower court's decision and change it.

APPELLATE COURT: Any court that hears *appeals*. The highest American appellate court is the Supreme Court of the United States.

BILL OF RIGHTS: The first ten amendments to the United States Constitution, limiting the power of the federal government over individual citizens and over the states.

BRIEF: Written statement by a lawyer giving the facts of a case and the reasons he thinks his side should win. In many American *appellate courts*, briefs must be presented in printed form.

CAPITAL CRIME: A *felony* of such a serious nature that it may be punished by a sentence of death. Murder, for example, is a capital crime in all states that have the death penalty.

CASE: A dispute that is taken to court; what lawyers argue about and judges decide.

CERTIORARI: A formal order by which a higher court, particularly the Supreme Court, brings a case up from a lower court for review (from the Latin). The full name is *writ of certiorari*.

CIVIL CASE: Any legal dispute that is not a *criminal case*. Typically, a dispute between private individuals.

CLERK: A court official who is in charge of the records of the court. The Clerk of the Supreme Court is the top administrative official on its staff. See also *law clerk*.

COMMON LAW: The law made by judges as they decide cases and build up *precedents*, as opposed to *statute* law made by *legislatures*.

CONSTITUTIONAL: Permitted by the U.S. Constitution.

CONVICTION: In a *criminal case*, a finding that the *defendant* is guilty.

COUNSEL: Lawyer; a trained man or woman who gives advice on legal questions and speaks in court for those involved in cases.

CRIME: Any act considered harmful to the public which is forbidden by law and made punishable by fine, imprisonment or death.

CRIMINAL CASE: A case brought by the government charging someone with a *crime*.

CROSS-EXAMINATION: Questioning of a witness by the lawyer for the opposing side.

DEFENDANT: The person against whom a lawsuit is brought. In a *criminal case*, the defendant is the person accused of a crime.

DISSENT: The view of a judge who disagrees with a majority of his fellow judges on how a case should be decided.

FEDERAL GOVERNMENT: The national or central government of a union of separate states. In the United States the federal capital is Washington, D.C.

FEDERALISM: System of government that divides powers between separate states and a central government, as in the United States.

FELONY: A serious crime, such as robbery or murder.

IN FORMA PAUPERIS: Method by which a poor person may have his case considered in a court, notably the Supreme Court, without having documents printed and without paying court fees (from the Latin).

JUDICIAL REVIEW: Examination by a court of a decision by government officials to see whether it was fair and legal. In the United States, courts have the power to review statutes to se whether they are *constitutional*, and it is in this special sense that people speak of the Supreme Court's power of judicial review.

JURISDICTION: The extent of a court's authority. For example, a court usually has jurisdiction only over certain kinds of cases and in a certain geographical area.

JURY: Group of citizens which listens to the evidence presented at a *trial* in court and, in a *criminal case,* decides whether the defendant is guilty or innocent.

LAW CLERK: A judge's assistant who helps on research, usually a young man or woman recently out of law school; or a young lawyer or student training at a law firm. See also *clerk*.

LAW REVIEWS: Magazines, mostly edited by students at law schools, which print articles on legal subjects.

LEGISLATURE: A body of men and women, representing the people, who meet to raise money for the government and to pass laws that are known as *statutes* or legislation.

MISDEMEANOR: A crime less serious than a *felony*.

OPINION: Statement by a judge of his reasons for a decision.

ORAL ARGUMENT: A lawyer's statements, made in person before a court, on how he thinks the case should be decided.

OVERRULE: To change an earlier decision. A court which refuses to follow one of its own *precedents* is said to overrule the previous case.

PETITION: A plea to a court. A petition for *certiorari*, for example, asks the Supreme Court to review a case.

PETITIONER: One who brings a *petition* to a court. Clarence Earl Gideon was the petitioner in the case of *Gideon v. Cochran*.

PRECEDENT: Rule made by a court in one case and usually followed in later cases of a similar kind.

PROSECUTOR: Lawyer employed by the government to bring *criminal cases* and, at each trial, to present the evidence against the *defendant*.

PUBLIC DEFENDER: Lawyer regularly employed by the government to represent persons accused of crime who are too poor to pay for their own lawyers.

RESPONDENT: The person on the other side of a case from the *petitioner*. In the case of *Gideon v. Cochran*, H. G. Cochran Jr. was the respondent.

REVERSE: To upset the existing decision in a case. An *appellate court* which thinks a case was wrongly decided reverses the lower court.

STATUTE: Law made by representatives of the people assembled in *legislatures*, such as Parliament in Britain and Congress in the United States.

TESTIMONY: Information given by a witness in court.

TRIAL: The proceeding in which the facts of a case are first examined in a court.

INDEX

Acheson, Dean, 37, 45

Adams, J. Frank, 178

Adamson v. California, 70

Agger, Carolyn, 47

American Bar Association *Journal,* 145

American Civil Liberties Union, 103, 108, 117–18, 127, 170–71

Amicus curiae briefs, 103, 104, 106–14

Appellate courts, state, 23

Arnold, Fortas and Porter (law firm), 47, 82

Article III, of United States Constitution, 25

Article VI, of United States Constitution, 27

Baxley, Allen, Jr., 97, 130, 152

Bay Harbor Poolroom, 7, 8, 50–52, 57, 80, 96, 98, 122–23, 169, 174–76, 179–80

Berlin, Gerald A., 106

Berryhill, Henry, Jr., 52

Betts, Smith, 74–75

Betts v. Brady, 34, 43, 46, 49, 53, 78–79, 125–26
    and *amicus curiae,* 103–04, 106–09, 111, 112–14

Black's dissent on, 135–36
    and brief written for Gideon, 82, 85–88, 90, 92–93
    Gideon's criticism of, 41
    and Jacob, Bruce Robert, 103–05, 110–11, 112–14, 128–30
    Supreme Court's 1942 decision on, 8, 12, 33, 40, 66, 74–76, 78–79, 123–24, 166
    Supreme Court's 1942 decision overruled, 138–43, 167

Bill of Rights, 68–71, 82, 86, 105, 127, 141

Black, Hugo L., 42, 63–66, 68–69, 74–76, 85, 122, 127
    quoted, 75, 128–29, 131, 138, 139–40, 143
    victory for, in Gideon case, 138–41, 143, 167

Block, Irwin J., 170–72

Brandeis, Louis D., 30, 37, 66

Brennan, William J., Jr., 76, 79, 121, 129, 137

Bryant, Farris, 151

Certiorari
    petition for, 31–33, 36, 42
    writ of, 31

Circuit Court, of Fourteenth Judicial Circuit of Florida, 9

Civil Liberties Union, American, 103, 108, 117–18, 127, 170–71

Civil War, 30, 67, 69, 166

Clark, Tom C., 79, 85, 121, 141

Clerk of Supreme Court, 37, 45, 121

Cochran, H. G., Jr., 6, 38

Common Law, 19

Communists, jailed in 1950's, 64–65

Congress, United States, 19, 30, 158–60

Constitution, United States, 7–9, 12, 62, 64, 147, 156, 160
and Bill of Rights, 68–71
double system of government created by, 20–21, 66
freedom of speech guaranteed by, 62, 64–65, 68, 70
jurisdiction of Supreme Court limited by, 25
meaning of, decided by Supreme Court, 26, 30

Cook, Henry, 50–52, 173–79

Counsel, right to, questions raised by, 59–77

Criminal Justice Act (1964), 151

Criminal law, complexity of, 80

Davis, John F., 39, 45–46, 121

Depression, economic, 72

Dissents, 134–35

Douglas, William O., 46, 76, 79, 122, 137–38, 141

Dred Scott case, 166

"Due process of law," 7, 8, 12, 26, 69–70, 75, 86, 113, 132, 157

Eisenhower, Dwight D., 121–22

Ely, John Hart, 82–86, 89–90, 93

England, 17–18

Erwin, Richard W., 39, 102–03, 105, 111, 145–46

Federal District Courts, 23

Federal law, 26–27

Federalism, 66, 91, 123–25

Felony, Gideon charged with, 88

First Amendment, 68, 70–71

First Circuit, United States Court of Appeals for, 24

Florida, Circuit Court of Fourteenth Judicial Circuit of, 9

Florida Supreme Court, 5, 29, 97, 111, 135–36, 170

Ford Foundation, 150, 159

Fortas, Abe, 45–49, 53, 98, 107, 162–63, 170
and brief written for Gideon, 81–82, 85–94, 112
Gideon represented by, 45–46, 48–49, 54, 78–82, 117–18, 122–27, 132
quoted, 79, 87, 123–27, 132

Fourteenth Amendment, 7–8, 69–71, 74–75, 81–82, 85–86, 91, 109, 113, 126–27, 139

Fourth Amendment, 68, 71, 77

Frankfurter, Felix, 63–64, 66–68, 70–71, 77, 80, 85, 164–65

199

and *Betts v. Brady* case, 34, 88,
110–11, 167–68
Fulton, Robert, 22

Georgieff, George, 103
Gideon, Clarence Earl, 3, 5, 28–29,
59, 152, 155–56, 159,
169–71
appearance of, 6, 95
autobiography of, 54–58
criminal record of, 56–57,
98–99, 112
felony charged against, 88
first page of petition by, 2
petition for certiorari by, 2, 33,
38–39, 43, 97
in prison, 94–100
represented by Fortas, 45–46,
48–49, 54, 78–82, 117–18,
122–27, 132
trial of, in Circuit Court, 10–11,
49–54, 86
verdict in retrial of, 179
Gideon v. Cochran, 6, 33, 39, 41,
43, 120–21, 138
Gideon v. Wainwright, 138, 150,
153, 155
Goldberg, Arthur J., 111, 121, 137

Harlan, John Marshall, 80, 85,
116, 121, 123–26, 131–32,
141–42
Harris, William E., 9, 50, 173,
176–78
Harvard Law School, 31, 106
Henderson, J. D., 175

Holmes, Oliver Wendell, Jr., 164
Hughes, Charles Evans, 135

"Incorporation" argument, 70,
85–86, 127, 141
In forma pauperis cases, 5, 6, 43
Interstate commerce, 21, 23, 26

Jacob, Bruce Robert, 39, 102–05,
110–14, 140
Gideon case argued by, 117–18,
123, 126, 128–30, 136
quoted, 119–20, 128–30,
135–36
Jefferson, Thomas, 62
Johnson, Lyndon B., 28, 48
Judicial review, by Supreme Court,
62
Jurisdiction, 24–26, 29

Kamisar, Yale, 89, 92, 126
Kennedy, John F., 28, 48, 111,
120–21, 151, 159
Kennedy, Robert F., 146
Krash, Abe, 81–82, 88–90, 93

Law clerks, 35
Legal Aid Society, 149
Legislatures, origin of, 19
Livingston, Robert R., 22

McCormack, Edward J., Jr., 106
McCrary, Robert L., Jr., 9, 11,
49–50, 52, 112, 171–172,
179

Mapp v. Ohio, 77, 79
Marbury v. Madison, 62
Marshal of Supreme Court, 119, 127
Marshall, John, 22–23, 41, 62
Mentz, George D., 109, 118, 130–32, 142
  quoted, 110
Mondale, Walter F., 105–06

Oral argument, 116–17

Panama City, Florida, 7, 9, 57, 87, 95, 99, 170, 172, 179
Parliament, British, 19, 72
Petition for certiorari, 31–33, 36, 42
Pitts, Duell, 175
Powell v. Alabama, 72–74
Precedents, 18–19, 65
Public defender, 148, 151

Quicksall v. Michigan, 142

Racial segregation, Supreme Court's decision on, 28, 62
Rankin, J. Lee, 108, 117, 127–28
Reapportionment Cases, 159–60
Right to counsel, 59–77
Rodak, Michael, Jr., 4–5, 6, 39
Rome, ancient, 18
Roosevelt, Franklin D., 46, 62, 122

Scottsboro boys, 73–74, 92, 156
Segregation, racial, Supreme

Court's decision on, 28, 62
Simon, Tobias, 170–72
Sixth Amendment, 68, 71–72, 74, 91, 113, 139
Solicitor General, 137
"Special circumstances," and due process, 9, 40–41, 53, 74–76, 82–84, 87, 92, 107, 113, 128–32
State courts, 23
  crimes punished by, 147
  free counsel provided by, 88–89, 92
  "special-circumstances" approach in, 84, 87
State law, 21, 25
States' rights, 67, 77, 104–05
Statutes, by legislatures, 20
Steamboat monopoly, Marshall's decision on, 22–23
Stetson Law School, 102
Stewart, Potter, 80, 121, 125, 127, 137
Story, Joseph, 27–28
Strickland, Ira, Jr., 51
Supreme Court, 35, 44, 64, 83, 159–67
  amicus curiae briefs filed in, 103, 104, 106–14
  argument before, 115–17, 119–20
  and *Betts v. Brady* case (1942), 8, 12, 33, 40, 66, 74–76, 78–79, 123–24, 166
  Chief Justice of, 36, 42
  Clerk of, 37, 45, 121

201

in conference, 41–43
as conscience of society, 159, 165–66
courtroom of, 119
dissents from majority opinions of, 134–35
Gideon case argued before, 117–18, 120–32
Gideon case decided by, 136, 138–43, 167
individual freedom upheld by, 158
judicial review by, 62
jurisdiction of, 24–26, 29
justices of, 17, 24, 35–37, 41–42, 61, 137, 158, 162
law clerks of, 35
Marshal of, 119, 127
Miscellaneous Docket of, 5–6
power of, 158
on racial segregation, 28, 62
responsibility of, 61
reversals of earlier decisions by, 65–66, 166
rules of, for paupers' cases, 4
Scottsboro boys' conviction reversed by, 73–74, 92

state court decisions reviewed by, 27–28
Supreme courts, state, 23

Temple, Ralph, 89, 93
"Third degree," 77
Thirteenth Amendment, 69
Trial judges, state, 23
Trial procedures, 50–51
Truman, Harry S, 32
Turner, W. Fred, 172–79

United States Courts of Appeal, 23–24
United States Reports, 142

Vinson, Fred M., 32, 37

Wainwright, Louie L., 138
Warren, Earl, 38, 45, 47, 76, 79, 120, 122, 127, 130, 150
Washington, George, 29
Wear, Ann, 110–11
White, Byron R., 37, 80, 121
Whittaker, Charles E., 61
Wolf v. Colorado, 71
Writ of certiorari, 31